Matthias Weinreich
„We Are Here to Stay"

**ISLAMKUNDLICHE UNTERSUCHUNGEN • BAND 285**

begründet
von Klaus Schwarz

herausgegeben
von Gerd Winkelhane

ISLAMKUNDLICHE UNTERSUCHUNGEN • BAND 285

Matthias Weinreich

# „We Are Here to Stay"

Pashtun Migrants in the Northern Areas of Pakistan

Photographs by Silvia Delogu

KLAUS SCHWARZ VERLAG • BERLIN

**Bibliografische Information der Deutschen Bibliothek**
Die Deutsche Bibliothek verzeichnet diese Publikation in der
Deutschen Nationalbibliografie; detaillierte bibliografische Daten
sind im Internet über *http://dnb.ddb*.de abrufbar.

**British Library Cataloguing in Publication data**
A catalogue record for this book is available from the British Library.
*http://www.bl.uk*

**Library of Congress control number available**
*http://www.loc.gov*

Cover shows Shina speakers waiting for the bus in Jaglot (Gilgit District).
You can contact the author at *mweinreich@hotmail.com*

*www.klaus-schwarz-verlag.com*

All rights reserved.
Alle Rechte vorbehalten. Kein Teil dieses Buches darf in
irgendeiner Form (Druck, Fotokopie oder in einem anderen
Verfahren) ohne schriftliche Genehmigung des Verlages
reproduziert oder unter Verwendung elektronischer Systeme
verarbeitet werden.

© 2009 by Klaus Schwarz Verlag GmbH
Erstausgabe
2. Auflage 2010
Herstellung: J2P Berlin
Gedruckt auf chlorfrei gebleichtem Papier
Printed in Germany
ISBN 978-3-87997-356-9 sowie 978-3-11-110410-2

## Table of Contents

Preface ........................................................................................................6

**Part 1** **Introduction**..................................................................13
1.1 Geographic and socio-linguistic setting................................13
1.2 Pashto speakers in the region................................................16

**Part 2** **The Migrants' Story**.....................................................
2.1 Pre-colonial period (until 1892): Early traces......................21
2.2 The Kashmiri-British colonial period (1892–1947):
 Moving into position............................................................. 24
2.2.1 Traders and craftsmen............................................................25
2.2.2 Farmers....................................................................................33
2.2.3 Other professions....................................................................38
2.3 Post-Partition period (after 1947):
 Showing strong presence........................................................40
2.3.1 Prior to the Karakoram Highway:
 A lead in trade and crafts.......................................................42
2.3.2 With the Karakoram Highway:
 Reaping the economic benefits..............................................53
2.3.2.1 Traders and smugglers............................................................55
2.3.2.2 Craftsmen.................................................................................65
2.3.2.3 Other occupations...................................................................70

**Part 3** **Pashto, Urdu and the others**......................................79
3.1 Using Pashto: Who, when and how......................................79
3.1.1 Facing the dialectal divide.....................................................82
3.1.2 Language maintenance: Means and opportunities..............89
3.2 Urdu as a communication tool..............................................90
3.3 Local languages: Attitudes, use and influence on Pashto..........93
3.4 Pashto as mother tongue: A pragmatic choice....................98

**Part 4** **To be Continued?**......................................................103
4.1 Form of migration................................................................103
4.2 Professional activities and geographical distribution...............104
4.3 Language situation and integration....................................107

**Annex**
 References..............................................................................115
 Table on the status of Pashto and local languages
 among Pashtun migrants......................................................119
 Map of the Karakoram Region............................................120

# Preface

Economically motivated migration of Pashto speakers from their original areas of settlement – situated on both sides of the present Pakistani-Afghan border (Durand Line) – to other regions of the Indian Subcontinent is an age-old phenomenon.[1] Its historical roots can be traced back to pre-Mughal times, when the loyal services of Pathan warriors were in high demand with the rulers in Delhi and the kingdoms further to the south. Nowadays larger Pakistani cities like Lahore, Quetta and especially Karachi pay host to hundreds of thousands of Pashtuns, working in all conceivable professions and trades. The majority of Pashto speakers came to these places over the last 20 to 30 years, some of them settling with their families, others migrating on a purely temporary basis. But Pashtun migration is far from limited to the big cities alone. With an ever increasing pace it is spreading practically all over the country. In fact, it is so prevalent that it would hardly be an exaggeration to state that there is not a single town left in Pakistan without its own Pathan trader, cobbler or teashop owner.[2]

What is true for the Pakistani lowlands, more and more also applies for the Karakoram high mountain region known under the name of Northern Areas. Pashtuns are relatively new to these places and represent only a small fraction of the area's total population. But their economic strength and growing social influence has already ensured them their very own, distinctive position within the ethno-linguistic groups present in this remote part of the country.[3]

---

1   In 1998 Pashtuns in Pakistan were estimated to comprise over 15% of the population, i.e. ca. 25 million people (Population Census Organisation). For Afghanistan there are no reliable recent numbers; before the beginning of the civil war in 1979 Pashto was the mother tongue of ca. 50% of the country's inhabitants (Skjærvø, p. 384). Detailed general information on Pashtun history and culture can be found in Caroe 1958.

2   According to Pakistan's Population Census Organisation in 1998 more than one million people originating from predominantly Pashto-speaking areas (NWFP and FATA) were living in the Provinces of Punjab, Sindh and Baluchistan.

3   The Pashto speakers living in the Northern Areas during the time of my research belonged to a variety of tribal, ethnic and social backgrounds and did not

The first researcher to recognise and systematically describe Pashtun migrants as an integral part of the Northern Area's population set-up was Hermann Kreutzmann, who also drew my attention to this subject. Later, in the framework of his investigation into the bazaar economies of Gilgit and Baltistan A. Dittmann (1995, 1997a, 1997b, 1998) published data pertaining to the economic role of Pashtun traders in the region. M. Sökefeld dealt with Pashtun migration while looking into the issue of group identity in Northern Pakistan (1997, 1998a), and devoted a separate article to popular stereotypes associated with the Pathans in Gilgit (1998b). And, last but not least, E. Bauer (1998) provided a short analysis of the migrants' language and socio-linguistic environment.

There are also a number of earlier works about the region (e.g. Biddulph 1880, Faggi; Ginestri 1977, Staley 1966, 1969) which contain notes on Pashtun presence in the Karakoram. However, there is no separate publication dealing with this subject in a more comprehensive way. The present book attempts to fill this gap by offering the reader an insight into some characteristic historical, economic and language-related aspects of Pashtun migration in the Northern Areas.[4] For this purpose the work is divided into four interconnected parts.

Part one gives an introduction into the geographic and socio-linguistic setting, including a short reference to Pashtun presence in Chitral and Kohistan.

Part two looks at the people as such, describing when and for what reason they arrived at their present place of living and what they were doing there in the mid 1990s. The aim of this chapter is to connect Pashtun migration with the socio-economic development of the area. The time-

---

perceive themselves as a homogeneous community. The only feature linking all of them was their common mother tongue, by the virtue of which most representatives of the area's other ethno-linguistic communities saw them as one group. This language-centred outside perception is also taken as the basis for the present study. Subsequently, the terms 'Pashto speaker(s)', 'Pashtun(s)' and 'Pathan(s)' are used as full synonyms and applied to every person who in the mid 1990s spoke Pashto as his or her mother tongue.

[4] The forerunners of this book are two separate articles published by the author (2001, 2005) in Garnik Asatrian's "Iran and Caucasus".

frame under consideration is the last 150 years, which, in accordance with the regional political milestones, is divided into pre-colonial, colonial and post-partition periods. In this overall context special attention is given to the decades following the opening of the Karakoram Highway.

Part three looks into the migrants' language situation, investigating their ways of communicating with each other and with members of their host communities. Besides describing how Pashto speakers in the Northern Areas handled the complexities of cross-dialectal communication, the chapter also covers their attitudes towards Urdu and local languages, and attempts to find an answer to the question why some migrant households were prone to change their original mother tongue while others were not.

Part four proposes a glimpse into the future, trying to define in which way the most characteristic trends linked to Pashtun migration to the area in the mid 1990s could develop over the coming decades.

An annex contains a map of the wider region as well as a table showing the status of Pashto and local languages among permanent Pathan migrants.

The actual study is supplemented by and interwoven with a number of childhood memories and life stories which the people I had the chance to interview in the field chose to share with me. Because all those interviewed were just ordinary people leading ordinary lives – traders, cobblers, tea boys, farmers and porters – one would not expect their reminiscences to include anything of extraordinary importance. Nevertheless, or, maybe exactly because of that, it was felt that quoting these simple stories would not only give a voice to the Pashtun migrants themselves but also involve the reader in the human dimension of the original research. For the same reason the text is accompanied by a series of portraits, photographs taken by my wife, Silvia Delogu, during our years in the Northern Areas.

Besides making use of written accounts the present study draws heavily on oral sources. The material was collected by me from people in the Northern Areas – both Pashtun migrants and representatives of other ethno-linguistic groups – during field work in the years 1993 to 1997.[5] Since the bulk of the data was obtained through direct inquiry, it may be helpful to provide an insight into the methodology applied. Most of the field work I conducted directly in Pashto; for Urdu and Shina the help of a local interpreter was employed. My main aim was to interview as many informants as possible looking for answers to sets of predefined questions. All these interviews were held in the form of casual conversations, during which I never used a questionnaire and always attempted to avoid the impression of somebody just interested in short and quick information. This somewhat indirect method was chosen, because previous experience had shown that straightforward inquiry could easily provoke misunderstandings and generate a negative attitude towards my work, thus influencing the reliability of the answers provided. For the same reasons I also very soon gave up my initial attempts to tape the conversations.

For the interviews two different sets of questions were used. The first set, which I employed with both Pashto and (to some extent) non-Pashto speakers, was connected to the personal and family history of the communication partners. Set two, which targeted only Pashtuns – normally the same persons as set one – aimed at finding out about the interviewee's language situation.

Besides looking for basic information regarding name, ethnic and tribal affiliation, religion, occupation, place of living and marital status I was also interested in a number of more complex issues like the origins of the person's forefathers, his level of mother tongue education, his personal linguistic abilities and preferences, the language use patterns within his household, with friends and neighbours, his relationship with representat-

---

5   From 1993 to 1995 my research was financed by the German Research Council (DFG) and integrated into the framework of the German-Pakistani Culture Area Karakoram (CAK) Project. Herewith I would like to take the opportunity to thank my then project supervisor Prof. Dr. Manfred Lorenz and my colleagues in the field Hermann Kreutzmann, Jens-Peter Jakobsen, Reinhard Fischer, Wolfgang Holzwarth and Erhard Bauer for their valuable help and advice. I would also like to express my gratitude to the German Research Council for its generous support.

*Abdul Qayyum, Shaban Ali and the author (right) during an interview*

ives of other ethno-linguistic groups. Requesting more than just superficial statements on these topics, which were for many speakers rather sensitive, was preconditioned on a relationship of mutual trust, which, in the given context, could normally only be established through repeated meetings and an open exchange of thoughts. It was mainly through the cultivation of such individual contacts, some of which resulted in personal friendships, that I was enabled to participate in a number of aspects of the migrants' life and substantiate the received statements with my own observations.

But, of course, the applied method also had its disadvantages. First of all, it was very time consuming, a fact which made itself specially felt in situations when a particular interviewee could not be seen on more than one occasion. And second, it did not give space for the collection of uninterrupted Pashto texts, with the consequence that all life stories quoted in this study are post-interview compilations rather than translations from directly recorded material.

An aspect of research, which remained, unfortunately, completely off-limits to me was the work with female informants. The traditional way of life prevalent among Pashto speakers (not only) in the Northern Areas precludes women from interaction with men not belonging to their family. Therefore, I was in no position to interview them or to confirm statements made on their behalf by male household members. It will, thus, be left to an interested female researcher to augment the present study with the Pashtun women's own perspective.

Finally, I have the pleasant task of extending thanks to those who contributed to the creation of this book.

First of all, I owe enormous gratitude to all my interviewees without whose engagement and goodwill the whole project would have never got off the ground. Besides them, Jelena Charlamowa (Berlin) provided crucial help and great encouragement during the initial stages of the study. Adam Nayyar (Islamabad) shared with me his intimate knowledge of the area and shaped my opinion on many ethnological and socio-linguistic issues. Caroline Taylor (Skopje) and Jason Brown (London) spared valuable time to correct my English, and Darko Jordanov (Geneva) was responsible for a number of helpful editorial comments.

Last, but by no means least, I am deeply indebted to my parents, Paul and Irma Weinreich, my wife, Silvia Delogu, and our daughter, Emily, for supporting me and putting up with me during the seemingly endless time this study was under preparation. I dedicate this book to them.

# Part 1

# Introduction

## 1.1 Geographic and socio-linguistic setting

As already suggested by the name, the Northern Areas of Pakistan are situated in the far north of the country. They encompass a high mountain territory of around 72,500 km², covering the greater part of the Karakoram range as well as western fringes of the Himalayas and eastern fringes of the Hindukush. Because of its dramatic landscape dotted with an impressive number of snow-capped mountain peaks, among them the Nanga Parbat, the Rakaposhi and the K2, this part of Northern Pakistan is often associated with the legendary Roof of the World.

Moving clockwise from their southern limits, the Northern Areas border upon Hazara, Kohistan and Chitral (all three part of Pakistan's North-West Frontier Province), the Wakhan District of Afghanistan, the Xinjiang Autonomous Region of the People's Republic of China, as well as upon Indian-administered and Pakistan-administered Kashmir.

Until recently the Northern Areas were divided into five administrative units: the Gilgit, Ghizar, Diamer, Skardu and Ganche Districts. In 2004 the Government of Pakistan announced the establishment of a sixth entity – Astor, centring around the homonymous valley in the east of Diamer. The present study will, however, continue to refer to the older administrative set-up, as this was the one in use at the time of the original research.

In the mid 1990s the Northern Areas consisted of around 600,000 inhabitants, with approximately 40,000 of them residing in Gilgit, the region's largest town, its administrative capital and its financial heart. The two other urban centres were Chilas and Skardu Town, headquarters of the Diamer and Skardu Districts respectively. Although urbanisation was, as in other regions of Pakistan, an ongoing process, the overwhelming

*Karakoram landscape*

majority of the population was still to be found in rural areas, in villages and larger settlements scattered oasis-like across the bottom of the bigger valleys and alongside the major roads.[6]

Even within a country endowed with an extraordinarily rich heritage of cultures and languages like Pakistan, the Northern Areas distinguished themselves by an unusual ethno-linguistic diversity.

In the mid 1990s one could find more than ten linguistically different population groups living on their territory. The three main sections, consisting of 150,000, 90,000 and 260,000 people respectively, were the speakers of the Dardic Shina, the isolated BurushaskiUnazHu HUIIIi, and the West Tibetan Balti. Because of their numbers, their prestige and their long-standing settlement history, these groups were generally regarded as the autochthonous inhabitants of the area.

Others had arrived at a later stage. Among them were the approximately 10,000 speakers of the East Iranian Wakhi, who had migrated in

---

6   For a comprehensive description of the area's geography and recent history see Kreutzmann 2005a.

the 19th century from the Wakhan corridor and settled in the Hunza and Ishkoman Valleys, and the around 27,000 speakers of the Dardic Khowar in Ghizar District who by language and culture were linked to neighbouring Chitral. Smaller groups included the less than 350 speakers of Domaaki in the Nager and Hunza Valleys, who were linguistically affiliated with languages of the Indian lowlands; the Uighurs residing in Gilgit Town who had fled in the 1950s from neighbouring Xinjiang; and the Gujur herders who had moved in from the southern mountain foreland and were now to be found close to high pastures in Diamer, Gilgit and Ghizar Districts.

While from a linguistic point of view some of the rural areas could be regarded as comparatively homogenous – Diamer and the south of Gilgit District predominantly Shina-speaking; Central Hunza and Nager Valleys predominantly Burushaski-speaking; and Ganche and Skardu Districts predominantly Balti-speaking – the urban centres Gilgit, Skardu and Chilas were the place where all ethnicities met.

During my work in the Northern Areas I observed that for a number of population groups linguistic boundaries were rather transparent. Thus, in areas of their speakers' compact settlement Shina, Burushaski, Balti and Khowar were not only employed as mother tongues, but also fully mastered as a second language by members of local minority groups. Moreover, some of these minority groups had adopted or were in the process of adopting the local majority language as their own mother tongue. In this way, all Kashmiris who had come to Gilgit in the 18th century had since long given up their idiom in favour of Shina; the Dooma (people traditionally working as blacksmiths and musicians) in Ghizar District had fully switched from their original Domaaki to Khowar or Shina, while the remaining Domaaki speakers in Nager and Hunza were in the process of moving to Shina or Burushaski; Kohistani-speaking households in Gilgit and Chilas were changing to Shina etc. This linguistic redefinition was by no means a recent process, or just limited to tiny minorities. In fact, numerous place names in the Karakoram suggest, that a large part of the territory now covered by Shina and Indus Kohistani must once have been Burushaski-speaking (Zoller, p. 19f).

The heterogeneity of the ethno-linguistic picture was mirrored by a similarly diverse religious set-up. While all inhabitants of the Northern Areas confessed Islam, they were divided into four major (and partly antagonistic) groups: Sunnites, Twelver Shiites, Ismailis and Nurbakhshis. At the same time, clear correlation between ethno-linguistic background and religious affiliation was the exception rather than the rule. Thus, a Shina speaker could be a Sunnite or a Shiite or an Ismaili, a Burushaski speaker a Shiite or an Ismaili, a Balti speaker a Nurbakhshi or a Shiite and so on.

The geographic distribution of the major persuasions was as follows: the Diamer District to both sides of the Indus, including the Darel-Tangir Valleys and the area surrounding Chilas, was completely Sunni. Around Gilgit, as well as in the Punyal and the Astor Valleys the population was Shia and Sunni mixed. Ismailis were mostly in Hunza and Yasin. Central Nager was entirely Shia, as were the Shigar Valley in the north and the villages in the south-east of Skardu District. And, last but not least, most of the people in Ganche belonged to the Nurbakhshi belief. Among the urban centres it was Gilgit, which with an approximate division of 45% Sunnites, 45% Shiites and 10% Ismailis (Dittmann 1998, p. 50) was confessionally the most diverse and which also had the biggest share of sectarian violence.

## 1.2 Pashto speakers in the region

Although Pathans were relative late arrivals to the Northern Areas, to the wider Karakoram/Eastern Hindukush region their migration was not a new phenomenon.

During the 15th and 16th centuries the lower parts of the Swat and the Dir Valleys as well as Bajaur, all areas once entirely occupied by non-Muslim speakers of Dardic languages, were conquered and settled by Muslim Pathans arriving from the south. From these places further religiously motivated inroads were made into the remaining Dardic territory. Sunni Islam was spread and with it came the Pathans and their language.

In the course of time, Pashtuns replaced or absorbed a large faction of the Dardic population in the upper parts of Swat and Dir and established settlement pockets in Indus Kohistan. By the mid 20th century Pashto had become the *lingua franca* of all these places (Barth, p. 6; Hallberg 1992b, p. 139; Decker, S. J., p. 77). Moreover, there are indications that in the 1950s most professional craftsmen in Indus Kohistan were Pashto-speaking; descendant families of early Pashtun preachers had occupied a top position in society and Pathan-Paracha entrepreneurs engaged in local trade (see Barth, pp. 6, 26 ff., 40 ff).

Further to the north-west, in Chitral, Pashto-speaking merchants had been active at least since the second half of the 19th century, when they were mainly involved in trade with Peshawar, Afghanistan and Turkistan. Their presence increased during colonial times and then again over the second half of the 20th century. In the 1960s Pathan entrepreneurs were estimated to control up to 85% of Chitral's total trade volume (Israr-ud-Din, p. 55). In the mid 1990s Pathans were to be found in Chitral Town and in Drosh, in villages along the Chitral river between Drosh and Arandu, in the Arkari, the Shishikuh and the Urtsun Valley as well as in Reshun and Mastuj (Decker, K.D., p. 20; Cacopardo, Alb., pp. 279, 286; Cacopardo, Aug., p. 234; Holdschlag, p. 4).

Estimates from the end of the 1980s set the number of mother tongue Pashto speakers at around 3,000 people, which made for approximately 1.2% of Chitral's total population (Decker K.D., p. 11). Besides this, Pashto was spoken by many members of local ethno-linguistic minority groups as second or third language and had replaced Khowar in its function as main *lingua franca* in Southern Chitral (Holdschlag, p. 4; Decker, K.D., pp. 38, 83).

Pashtun migration in the Northern Areas dates back at least to the 19th century. The earliest written sources mention itinerary traders in places bordering with Chitral and settler households in valleys to the north of Indus Kohistan. In the course of the 20th century, the number of Pashto speakers increased significantly, first in the 1920s and 1930s and then again after Partition, reaching its temporary peak in the years following the opening of the Karakoram Highway.

In the mid 1990s Pashtun migrants could be encountered in all of the area's five districts. While working predominantly as traders, craftsmen and in the service sector, they were mostly concentrated in the urban centres; outside of Gilgit, Chilas and Skardu their presence was usually limited to centrally located market places and to certain villages in parts of the Ghizar, Diamer and Gilgit Districts. Almost all Pashtun migrants were adherents of Sunni Islam, some, very few individuals belonged to the Shiite sect.

In accordance with their way of life the Pathans in the Northern Areas could be divided into two types: temporary/seasonal and permanent migrants. People of the first type had retained their connections with their place of origin, at which they used to visit their families on a regular basis. In the Northern Areas these migrants lived in temporary households (Psh. *dēra* "temporary dwelling-place") which they normally shared with male relatives or friends. The second type of migrants had left their place of origin for good and had made the Northern Areas their new home, establishing their own permanent family household (Psh. *kōr* "place where one stays with one's family") there.[7]

As far as their language was concerned, the migrants represented a vast variety of Pashto dialects. Besides this, many of them were also fluent in one or more of the local languages. A number of rural households were even affected by mother tongue change. Other migrants, however, did not speak anything else than Pashto and a little Urdu. Interestingly, and differently from Chitral and Kohistan, there was no district or region within the Northern Areas where Pashto functioned as a *lingua franca*.

According to data issued by the Pakistani Government (quoted after Kreutzmann, 2005b, p. 2), back in 1981 Pashto speakers constituted 0.8% (= approximately 4590 persons) of the area's total population. At the same time, the proportion between Pathans in urban centres and Pathans in rural areas was 6:1.[8] A survey made in 1991 by H. Kreutzmann, which,

---

[7] Throughout this study the rendering of Pashto words and phrases follows the system applied in Skjærvø 1989; names of persons and places are given in a simplified transcription.

[8] A further break-down of the 1981 data by the administrative units of that time shows the following: Pashtuns constituted 0.72% of the population of Gilgit District (228,000 inhabitants), 0.08% of Baltistan District (223,000 inhabitants) and 2.24% of Diamer District (123,000 inhabitants).

however, excluded Diamer District, showed approximately 1660 speakers.[9]

Taking into consideration that the fast economic growth of the region in the 1980s and 1990s attracted a significant amount of new arrivals, I would estimate the number of Pashtun migrants present in the Northern Areas in the mid 1990s at around 5,000 to 5,500 people, which would have counted for about 0.8-0.9% of the total population.

---

9   Kreutzmann estimated that in 1991 Pashto speakers constituted 0.25% of the population of Skardu District (145,569 inhabitants), 0.7% of Ghizar District (95,329 inhabitants) and 0.3% of Gilgit District (177,458 inhabitants) (Kreutzmann 2005b, pp. 10-11).

# Part 2

# The Migrants' Story

## 2.1 Pre-colonial Period (until 1892): Early traces

For most of the 19th century what are now called the Northern Areas could be characterised as a conglomerate of more or less independent, economically backward valleys situated on the extreme north-western periphery of Kashmir and British India. Some of these valleys, among them the northern principalities of Hunza, Nager and Yasin were ruled by hereditary autocrats. Others like the southern mini-republics of Tangir, Darel and Chilas were governed by an elected council of elders.

The life of the area's population was largely dependent upon archaic, subsistence-level agriculture and livestock rearing. Surplus production of food, if it occurred at all, was mostly spent on collective feasting and, predominantly in the autocratically ruled valleys, on organizing the construction and maintenance of an elaborate irrigation system. In the council-governed valleys of the south, non-agrarian sources of income were virtually non-existent. In the equally poor northern principalities, the ruling nobility used to supplement their meagre takings by plundering passing caravans and selling captured travellers and their own subjects into slavery.[10]

The area's precarious economic conditions were echoed by a volatile political situation. Over the centuries, relations between the valleys alternated between long-term feuds and short-term alliances, often driven by conflicts involving powerful regional neighbours like Tibet, China, Kashmir and Chitral. By the middle of the 19th century, interests asserted by an increasingly dominant Kashmir had once again plunged the area into a situation of permanent insecurity, complemented by periodic outbreaks

---

10  For a detailed analysis of the area's socio-economic situation in the 19th and early 20th century see Staley 1969.

of straight-forward warfare. At around the same time, Britain and Russia started to turn their attention towards the still widely unexplored region, which because of its location on the very seam of their territorial interest, had suddenly acquired strategic importance in the two colonial empires' newly emerging 'Great Game'.

The earliest records mentioning a regular Pashtun presence in the area date back to these troubled times. The first notes available to us can be found in a British military report, later published by the Royal Geographical Society. Its author, Munpool Meer Moonshee, was one of the famous 'Pundits', locally recruited agents trained by the Army's Intelligence Service to collect information in countries and places where it was deemed safe for only 'natives' to go to. In the early 1860s Munpool Meer was commissioned to travel, disguised as a trader, from Peshawar through Chitral and Wakhan up to the city of Kashghar in East Turkistan (today's Xinjiang Region of China). Besides surveying the area on his way, he also enquired about everything which could be of military or commercial interest to his employers. The information Munpool Meer was able to collect about the situation in eastern Chitral and Ghizar, places at that time completely out of reach for European travellers, also included some reference to trading activities of merchants from Peshawar, Afghanistan and Dir, a valley to the south of Chitral, which the author, following the practice of his time, referred to as 'Yaghistan' (Munpool Meer, p.133).

According to Munpool Meer's sources some of the more adventurous Yaghistani entrepreneurs would in the course of their seasonal business trips to Chitral also make detours to Ghizar's Yasin Valley, where they used to trade with horses as well as exchange salt, iron, cloth and all kinds of haberdashery for local agricultural products and slaves. These journeys were described as dangerous and physically demanding, but also rather profitable, especially with regards to the advantageous purchase of young female serfs.

Further mention of Pathans in the Karakoram region is made in John Biddulph's famous work "Tribes of the Hindoo Koosh". Major (later Colonel) Biddulph, who combined his military profession with a vocation for academic study, served in the second half of the 1870s as the first permanent British representative in what later was to become the 'Gilgit Agency'. In his book, which is based on material collected during a prolonged stay in the area, he provides an impressive amount of detailed and well systematised information on the distribution, history, customs and languages of the different ethnic groups with which he came in contact. To Pashto speakers Biddulph refers only in passing, but on three different occasions. First, while describing the prevalent commercial situation in the already mentioned Yasin Valley, he characterises the place as being "chiefly occupied by Kaka Khel traders from Peshawar". Further on he typifies the Chilas region in present day Diamer district, as a "traditional stronghold of mullahs from Swat". And, last but not least, in a table illustrating the "distribution of castes" in Chilas and the Darel and Tangir Valleys Biddulph records 'Pathans' besides traditional ethnic groups like 'Shin', 'Dom' and 'Yashkun' (Biddulph, pp. 10, 15, 34).

Biddulph's allusion to religious activities of mullahs from Swat in Chilas region was later echoed by Karl Jettmar (1960, p. 134; 1961, p. 81, 87) who, on the basis of ethnological and historical data, linked the influence of Pashtun missionaries to the conversion of the population of Indus Diamer to Sunni Islam.[11] In connection with this, the information provided in Biddulph's table can be taken as evidence for the existence of early Pathan settler households in the same area.[12]

With these rather scarce notes the written references to Pashtun presence in the Northern Areas before 1892 seem to be exhausted. Unfortunately, they can not be complemented with any oral recollections, as dur-

---

11  An early reference to the deeds of Pashtun clerics in that area can be found in the historical account "Tarikh-i Murassa", composed by Afzal Khan Khatak (ca. 1662–1748). While describing a religious campaign under the leadership of Akhund Chalak, student of Akhund Panju (d. 1631), directed against the "unbelievers of Chilas" the author narrates: "... and as they [Akhund Chalak and his war party] came to the Indus, there was neither boat nor raft. They twisted a few ropes out of tamarisk twigs, used them to lash branches together in a 'woven fence' and fashioned a raft. He [Akhund Chalak] then sent his war party across... They successfully carried out the battle for the Faith, took prisoners and came back by the same woven structure" (quoted after Holzwarth, p. 124).

12  As we shall see in chapter 2.2.2. such an interpretation of Biddulph's data will also be supported by later sources.

ing my research I was not able to gather reliable information dating back beyond the 1900s.

In any case, the sparseness of written material available on the subject seems to indicate that until the end of the 19th century Pashtun migration to the Northern Areas – with the prominent exception of Indus Diamer – was nothing but a hardly noticeable fringe phenomenon.

## 2.2 The Kashmiri-British colonial period (1892–1947): Moving into position

One of the most active regional military powers in the 19th century was Kashmir, an independent state to the south-east of the Karakoram, ruled by a dynasty of Dogra princes. Since their installation on the throne following the break-up of the Sikh Empire in 1846 the Dogras were entertaining close political links with British India. Already in the beginning of the 1840s the principality of Baltistan, containing the present day districts of Skardu and Ganche, had been invaded by a Sikh army; soon afterwards it was incorporated into Kashmir. Over the following decades the Dogras and their British allies succeeded in bringing most of the remaining Karakoram under their supremacy. The final step in the colonial conquest of the region was taken in 1891/92 with the subjection of the principalities of Hunza and Nager by a British expedition force.[13]

From 1901 onwards, the present day districts of Ghizar, Gilgit and most of Diamer constituted the so called 'Gilgit Wazarat', with Gilgit Town as its administrative centre. For the first three and a half decades of its existence the Wazarat was administered by Kashmir with active political and military support from the British, represented by a permanent Political Agent in Gilgit. In 1935 the Dogras leased the area – originally for a period of 60 years – to British India, which until the independence of the Subcontinent in 1947 took charge of it under the name of Gilgit Agency. The present day districts of Skardu and Ganche were, as part of

---

13 A detailed description of the Dogras' military expeditions to Baltistan, Diamer and Gilgit can be found in A. H. Dani's "History of Northern Areas of Pakistan". For a vivid account of the short, but fierce Hunza-Nager campaign see "Where three Empires Meet" by E. F. Knight.

Baltistan, merged with Kashmiri administered Ladakh in 1901 and remained under direct Dogra rule until autumn 1947.

In order to safeguard their freshly acquired possessions and to underpin their long-term strategic interests in the area the new colonial overlords stationed small but permanent military contingents in strategically located places such as Gilgit, Gupis, Chilas and Skardu. While the Gilgit Wazarat was directly administered by Kashmir (and later by the British), other valleys, like Hunza, Nager or Darel remained under their titular rulers or elected councils of elders, whose powers were, however, limited to matters of internal affairs.

The forceful pacification of the valleys, completed in the 1890s, was over the next decades supported by a whole range of well-conceived administrative measures. The main issue the new rulers focused on was the military and economic integration of the area into the wider region. An important move in this direction was the creation of a reliable communication link with Kashmir. This was achieved by widening and strengthening the traditional route via the Astor Valley, over the Burzil Pass to Srinagar. Further actions taken by the colonial administration included the building of bridges and roads within the area, reforms of the tax system and the development of fallow land. All these measures, as well as public construction and the already mentioned establishment and maintenance of military stations, led to an increased circulation of resources, turning central settlements like Gilgit and Gupis into attractive places for trade, business and employment.

### 2.2.1 Traders and craftsmen

Among the first to profit from the improving economic situation under Kashmiri-British supremacy were the merchants already operating in the area. It can safely be assumed that it was thanks to the contacts they had established in the western valleys during pre-colonial times that Pashtun traders operating via Chitral remained, for many years to come, at the forefront of entrepreneurs catering to the commercial needs of today's Ghizar District. During the time of my research some representatives of old-established Pashtun families settled in Gupis, Taus and Gilgit were still able to recall details connected to the early years of their ancestor's activities in the area. *Sarwar Khan*, a ca. 75-year-old textile merchant from Gilgit, remembered the origins of his family business as follows:

"My grandfather *Rahim Dad* was the first of us to arrive to these places. He came from a poor Paracha family in Dir. His most valuable possession was a pair of mules, which he drove every year from Chitral over the Shandur [the main pass between Chitral and the Northern Areas] to the settlement of Gupis. There he traded with goods he had brought from Dir or bought in the bazaar of Chitral. It was a very difficult journey. My father *Mohammad Daud*, May Allah be pleased with him, often told me how, as a young boy, he had accompanied his father on these arduous trips. He didn't go to school like the children of today; instead he had to help with the mules. His mother remained in the village and he saw her only during the winter. Every year they left home in spring and bought salt, tea and cloth in Chitral Town. Then they set out for Gupis. Normally they were part of the first caravan to cross the Shandur. Often the route was still covered with snow and it was very difficult to lead the animals across the narrow paths. Usually they made several such trips each season, as they had to earn enough money for the family back home. When the passes were closed in winter there was no work at all.

Later, my grandfather set up his own shop in Gupis, nothing but a small kiosk made of planks, in what is now the Old Bazaar, in a place he had rented from a local farmer. His stall was one of the first Pashtun-owned shops in the local market. Unlike today there were very few of us in Gupis and the bazaar was also much smaller. Best of all I remember Uncle *Mohsin*, a friend of my father's from his native village, who was a Mochi and worked as shoemaker and saddler. My father had married my mother in the village and later brought her to Gupis. I was around ten years old at that time and my brother even younger. After settling in Gupis my father was earning well and did not make the trip with the animals across the pass himself anymore. My grandfather went back to the village where he died.

Our first house in Gupis still belongs to us; but the old shop has long since been replaced with a much larger one in the New Bazaar. Since my mother's arrival all of us were staying in Gupis the whole year. Both my maternal uncles helped us with the trade in summer. One of them brought goods through Chitral while the other sold them to the farmers of Yasin and Punyal. The locals normally had no money, so we took woollen fabric, butter and goat hair instead. With these earnings my uncles went back to Chitral and Dir before the first snow of the season. My brother and I helped in the shop in Gupis. It was difficult because everybody wanted to buy our goods but nobody had much for exchange. So we wrote up their debts and when it was time for them to pay, people used to get angry since they couldn't give us anything. My father acquired some farmland from one of these men, because he was so heavily indebted to us. However, we didn't work the land ourselves; instead we leased it out to the former owner.

Besides his business in Gupis my father also used to go to Gilgit for trade. I normally went along with him. At first we just brought goods to Gilgit, mostly salt and fabric, but then we rented a shop in the town and stayed for the winter. During the cold season business was better there than at our old place, as in the snow and the ice no one carried goods from Gupis to the valleys and even in Gupis itself trade was very slow. Besides this, unlike the farmers of Ghizar, people here in Gilgit often paid cash right away, so we didn't have to go through the troubles connected to writing up the debt. However, a trip from Gupis to Gilgit was a rather onerous undertaking. Back then the path was much more difficult to negotiate as compared to the road of today, and it would take us several days to reach our destination.

Later, when I was around fifteen, we moved completely to Gilgit, to what is now the neighbourhood of Amperi, close to the shrine

*Wholesaler and guest in Gilgit's Raja Bazaar*

of *Sayed Sher Afzal*. My uncles stayed back in Gupis. Uncle *Fazil* took over our old shop and Uncle *Burhan* took care of the deliveries from Chitral. Back then the bazaar in Gilgit was very small. We had a shop in Raja Bazaar, where other Pashtuns from our area also worked. However, the best shops at that time belonged to the Hindus and the Kashmiris. They were concentrated close to the place the Friday Mosque is now located. By-and-by, more Pashtuns from Dir and Bajaur came over, among them such well known personalities as the blacksmith *Lala Khan*, who died childless in the 1950s, *Payanda Khan* with his General Store and the second-hand dealer *Mohammad Khan*, the father of *Yunus Kabari*, who now runs the automobile spare-parts shop in Airport Bazaar."

Gilgit, February 1994

Gupis, mentioned by *Sarwar Khan* as the place of his family's first permanent shop, was at his grandfather's time the most important settlement on the Chitral – Gilgit Route. This importance was connected to its favourable geographical location. Firstly, Gupis stood on the thoroughfare of all traffic to and from the Shandur Pass. And, secondly, it oversaw the entry into the fertile Yasin Valley, which over the Darkot and Boroghil Passes connected to the commercially and militarily significant Wakhan Route.

In the mid 1990s Gupis was a thriving township, featuring several thousand inhabitants, three schools and two bazaars. The Gupis of the early 1900s can easily be imagined as a small village consisting of a dozen or so houses surrounded by their fields and supplemented by a bazaar site nearby. Nevertheless, there is little doubt that already from the very beginning of regional trade Gupis, thanks to its central location, will have figured as the most suitable place for the establishment of a permanent market catering to the needs of the surrounding valleys. Moreover, it was surely the same geographic features which induced the Kashmiri administration to station a small military contingent just outside the village's perimeter.

Once the troops were there, regionally operating traders will have been commissioned to provide the little post with food and other supplies, the soldiers themselves will have spent part of their pay on the goods and services on offer in the bazaar and local villagers will have found employment in construction and all kinds of service jobs. It can thus be expected that over the years, increased economic development deriving from the establishment of the military station should have encouraged more and more traders to chose Gupis as their operational base. And indeed, a British colonial source dating back to the mid 1920s indicates the existence of six permanent shops in the local bazaar (Kreutzmann 1995, p. 114), one of which may have belonged to *Sarwar Khan's* family. Of course, the mentioned amount of businesses does not strike one as excessively high. However, considering, on the one hand, the backwardness of the area in general economic terms, and, on the other, the fact that resident merchants were normally complemented by mobile traders the like of *Sarwar Khan's* maternal uncle, this modest number can be interpreted as indicating a significant increase of business activities in Ghizar District as compared to pre-colonial times.

In fact, *Sarwar Khan* was not the only person interviewed who was able to recall the early days of Pashtun trade in the area. A number of elderly inhabitants of Yasin and Punyal still vividly remembered Pathan merchants travelling through the valleys and trading with the local population. These strangely clad travellers were often the only foreigners one could hope to see during the entire year and the simple things they had on offer stood for everything desirable from the mysterious world outside. With the passage of time the more successful Pashtun traders, like *Sarwar Khan's* grandfather, opened permanent shops in Gupis, where they shared market space with merchants from Kashmir, who had reached Ghizar not through the Shandur Pass, but via Astor and Gilgit. Less fortunate entrepreneurs continued to pick up their wares from Gupis, carrying them on mules or on their back from village to village in search of new customers.[14]

As is evident from the *Sarwar Khan's* recollections, not all potential buyers had the ready resources – money or, more often, barter goods like animal or field products – to pay for the offered items. In consequence, many a penniless farmer found himself in the unhappy position of being bound to the busy traders. There is little doubt that this situation was favoured by the merchants' almost unconditional readiness to sell goods on credit. Such business practises – at the time of my research still very common, particularly in rural areas – were often held by local interviewees against the Pashtun traders. Moreover, it was alleged that in former times some of the more ruthless Pathan entrepreneurs even used to supplement their range of goods on sale with raw opium, thus maximising business returns by making their clients physically dependent on their services. In this context one elderly man from Yasin Village related to me with still clearly perceptible bitterness, how his father was step-by-step selling out

---

14  For the south of the Gilgit Wazarat, probably present-day Diamer, British colonial sources register "traders from the Indus Valley districts of Kolai and Palas [who] bring up their goods from village to village for sale." (General Staff India 1928, quoted after Kreutzmann 2005b, p. 16). It is not excluded that also these merchants were Pashto speakers, members of Pathan communities settled in Indus Kohistan, as representatives of autochthonous groups from these places normally did not engaged in long-distance trade.

the family's possessions just to be able to support his addiction with supplies regularly delivered by a Pathan.

Thus it appears that the relationship between the traders and the local population was not always an easy one, especially when it came to issues connected to payment. Pashtun merchants, who on occasion also acted as money lenders, were well known for collecting outstanding dues up to the last copper coin; and as they did not belong to the local community, there was little hope for mediation by influential relatives or respected village elders. Sometimes liabilities could only be cleared through the sale of property. However, in such cases the debtors normally ensured that arable land, in short supply throughout the whole area, remained within the local community. Instances of direct transfer of agricultural fields to non-locals, as happened in the case of *Sarwar Khan's* father, were the exception rather than the rule.

Lucrative trade combined with the possibility of obtaining land – be it on temporary lease or through outright sale – for the establishment of private houses or shops in the bazaar, gave the impetus to Pashto-speaking traders in Gupis to change from seasonal presence to permanent migration. The beginning of this process must have been a rather modest one, since, according to local sources, until the 1930s the settlement counted only two to three resident Pashto-speaking families. However, later years will have seen a stronger increase, as interviewees reported the existence of more than a dozen permanent Pashtun households in Gupis by the time of Independence in 1947.[15]

With Gupis as their new base, the more adventurous among the Ghizar traders soon started to extend their activities to Gilgit Town, the area's

---

15   The increased presence of Pathan traders in the area after 1935 might also be connected to the fact that in that year the Amir of Afghanistan closed the border between Badakhshan and Chitral. As by this measure merchants from Dir and Bajaur were prevented from further participation in the Turkistan trade, some of them may have redirected their efforts to Ghizar and Gilgit. Besides this, in 1936 the British administration facilitated the permanent settlement of outsiders in Gilgit Town and other parts of the Agency by granting local owner-cultivators the right to sell a certain percentage of their property (Sökefeld 1998b, pp. 285, 297).

administrative centre. One reason for this expansion may well have been the annual winter slack in Gupis market, as stated by *Sarwar Khan*. But on the other hand, the incentive of a faster turnover linked to the presence of more and richer customers will also have played an important role.

Over the years a number of Pashto-speaking Ghizar traders settled permanently in Gilgit, where in the mid 1990s their descendants were still forming the heart of the local merchants' community.[16] The first shops of these Pathan business pioneers were almost exclusively located in what is now called Raja Bazaar, a trade cluster to both sides of Gilgit's exit route to Ghizar. Their houses were concentrated in the adjoining neighbourhoods of Majini Mohalla and Amperi; the latter at that time nothing but a small village just outside the town's perimeter. Whereas in Ghizar Pashtun traders had enjoyed a clear edge in the market on account of their transport monopoly over the Shandur Pass, once in Gilgit they came into a direct conflict of interest with merchants from Kashmir and Punjab, most of them of Hindu or Sikh persuasion. Not only that these businessmen may have been favoured by their compatriots and co-religionists working in the colonial administration, they also benefited from the fact that their purchase bases were more closely located to the main production centres of British India and therefore their goods could be bought cheaper and transported faster along the comparatively well-developed trade route over the Burzil Pass. According to the recollections of some older interviewees, in Gilgit Town the ensuing commercial competition between both trader groups led to a rough division of offered goods and services, in which Pashto-speaking entrepreneurs mostly concentrated on the sale of salt, leather goods, metal products, mules, horses, blankets and Turkistani silk. Besides this, they organised transport operations within the region and continued to purchase agricultural products.

Whatever the compulsions of the market, Gilgit bazaar already at that time seems to have been synonymous with good business. It is thus not surprising that Staley estimated that towards the end of the colonial peri-

---

16  According to Sökefeld (1998b, p. 285) the majority of Pathan traders who operated in Gilgit before Partition belonged to the villages Mayar and Miankali in Jandul, now part of district Dir, but formerly belonging to Bajaur.

od there were already about 25 Pashtuns, traders and most probably also craftsmen, active in Gilgit Town (Staley 1966, p. 249, quoted after Kreutzmann 1989, p. 187).

As the family history of *Sarwar Khan* indicates Pashto speakers operating in Ghizar – and later on also in Gilgit – often belonged to the occupational groups of mule breeders (Parachas) and leatherworkers (Mochis). In their places of origin members of these groups, traditionally excluded from land ownership, were eking out a living as muleteers, petty traders and artisans. During the second half of the 19th century many of them were leaving their villages in search of better employment opportunities. Their specialised professional skills enabled them to easily find work as transporters and artisans in the region's upcoming urban centres, as well as to successfully engage in local and regional trade. The fact that back home Parachas and Mochis had no fields of their own, might explain why entrepreneurs like *Sarwar Khan's* father and grandfather did not exhibit any special interest in working the land made over to them by their defaulters, but were leasing it instead to local tenants. Another illustration of this approach towards agriculture is a case reported for the settlement of Bassin, a few kilometres west of Gilgit Town, where in the mid 1930s the Ghizar traders *Muhammad Daud* and *Mahbub Khan* had acquired a significant portion of farm land, which, until their descendants sold it in the 1970s, was cultivated on an annual revenue basis by local Shina speakers.

## 2.2.2 Farmers

While most of the traders saw in their newly-acquired fields nothing but a profitable investment commodity, for other migrant Pashto speakers arable land represented the very source of their livelihood. An early indication of the existence of such peasant-settlers can be found in an assessment report prepared by the Kashmiri Settlement Officer *Thakur Singh* and published in 1917 by the administration of Gilgit Wazarat. The document was providing data essential for the planning of taxation according to land use. In a related table the author enumerated not less than 52 chargeable Pashtun households, located in an area, nowadays roughly covered by the south of Gilgit District and parts of Diamer, including the Astor Valley (Thakur Singh, p. 46).

One would probably not go wrong to assume that these 52 settler families were somehow connected to the Pathans mentioned more than three decades earlier in Biddulph's "distribution of casts" table. Moreover, additional evidence for the existence of Pathan households in the same area was given by members of the Second German Hindukush Expedition, who during their work in southern Diamer in the mid 1950s came across a number of farmers, ancestors of religious preachers or their military followers (Jettmar 1960, p. 122, 133; 1961, p. 81, 87).

Considering all these indications, it was rather surprising, that when I visited the same places in the mid 1990s, there seemed to be only a handful of these early Pashto-speaking households left. Among the few Pashtun peasants I encountered was *Muhammad Isa*, a ca. 70-year-old villager from Tarishing near Rattu in the upper Astor Valley, who told me the following about the origins of his family:

> "My grandfather and his brother came to this place about 90 years ago. They were originally from Swat, where they had killed two men from the local Khan's clan in a land dispute. Then they had fled the valley in fear of revenge. They came to Kashmir in the service of the English. After some time they were told by a man from Astor that one could get land in his native region. They married the daughters of that man and settled here. My grandfather and his brother were good, hard-working farmers and later they were able to acquire more farmland. My father inherited our fields, his two cousins the ones of his uncle.
>
> Both, my grandfather and his brother died in old age. They were well-respected men in the village. However they never really learnt Shina and always spoke Pashto with each other. They even taught Pashto to their wives. I too learnt the language from them but I cannot speak it properly anymore. My children speak no Pashto. It has no importance for them. Although they call themselves 'Pathan', they do so only because Pashtuns are having an

*Old farmer from Astor Valley*

increasing influence here in the mountains. So, they are happy to be associated with them. Other families here in the valley are also descendents of Pashtuns, like *Sardar's* family in Churit [a settlement in the upper Astor Valley] and *Yusuf Khan's* family in Astor Village. However, none of them speaks Pashto any more, their language now is Shina."

Astor Village, March 1995

Sensitized by this family story I started to search for other Pashtun households, which had also given up their original mother tongue in favour of the language of their host community. Over the months to come, local informants drew my attention to a number of such cases, among them families in Hudur Valley (Diamer District), the village of Pakora (Ishkoman Valley, Ghizar District) as well as in and around Chilas. In all these places people still identified their ancestors as 'Pathans' but now used the local majority languages (Shina or Khowar) as their mother tongue.[17] From the memories they shared with me about how their forefathers had come to the Northern Areas it appeared that the example of *Muhammad Isa's* family could be taken as rather typical for the destiny of many early Pashto-speaking farmer-settlers: After a (voluntary or involuntary) break-up with their original home community the migrants (missionaries, their military followers and blood revenge refugees) put down roots in a new place by linking themselves, sometimes also trough marriage, to a local clan. Subsequently, most households founded in this way assimilated (at least linguistically) to their new surroundings in the course of two to three generations.

There is little doubt, that this rather rapid adaptation process will have had its fair share of responsibility for the 'disappearance' of most of the Pathan farmer households mentioned by *Thakur Singh* and the German Hindukush Expedition. However, this process did obviously not work for every rural settler.[18] During the time of my research there were still a number of Pashtun farmer families, who, even after staying for several

---

17 A similar case was described by S. Nejima (p. 408 ff.) for the upper part of Ghizar Valley. There, local Khowar speakers referred to themselves as 'Walie' and reported to be of Pathan Kaka-Khel origin, tracing the home of their forefathers all the way back to Mardan (now NWFP, to the north-east of Peshawar).

18 For a more detailed discussion of the issue of mother tongue change among Pashtun migrants see chapter 3.4.

generations in the Northern Areas did not show signs of giving up their original mother tongue. One of this 'resistant' households I found in Chatorkhand, a village in the lower part of Ishkoman Valley (Ghizar District). The head of the family, the ca. 75-year-old *Abdul Latif* took considerable pride in explaining to me that all of his ancestors had been of "real Pashtun stock". He also insisted that his children and grand-children were still in full command of Pashto, a claim fully corroborated by my own observations.

The history of *Abdul Latif's* family is rather unique in as much as, differently from other Pashtun migrants, his father arrived in the area on explicit invitation and under the direct protection of the British:

"Our father came from Swat. His family was closely related to the Wali, the local ruler there. One day my father had a dispute with the Wali's brother about some land which had earlier been promised to our family. The Wali sided with his brother and a fight ensued. My father and his people killed some of the Wali's men. The ruler took away all my father's land and swore revenge. My father was then compelled to leave his home. He went with his wife and some of his men to Peshawar where he placed himself in the service of the English. However, he didn't want to live in Peshawar or Punjab. He was apprehensive that the Wali's men would track him down there.

The English invited my father to Gilgit, promising him land and protection. He accepted and initially made his home in Amperi. My elder brother, *Abdul Qayyum*, was born there. It must have been about 80 years ago since my brother is that old now. The ruler of Ishkoman then gave our family some land in Chatorkhand. This deal had been mediated by the English. In those days no one wanted to live in the Ishkoman Valley. There was plenty of good land available but hardly anyone was taking care of it. Later many people settled in Ishkoman, even Parachas from Bajaur and Dir, who came as traders and now have shops in Imit [a settlement north of Chatorkhand]. One of their sons is in charge of the Government Guest House there and they opened a shop in Chatorkhand, too.

My father was never interested in trade. That was something for the Parachas. He was a real Pashtun and that's why he was a farmer. The soil here is fertile, we have enough water and also fruit trees grow in abundance. With the passage of time, our family acquired more and more farmland. We even own some land in Imit now. My brother and I have always worked in the fields. Our neighbours used to regard us with curiosity and wonder: 'Pathans, who work the land?' Well they knew only the traders, not the real Pashtuns – which we are. *Abdul Qayyum*, my older brother, still farms the land himself, but a great deal of it is now on rent. Later, I found work with the police. This service brings me a regular pension. My nephews used to help in the fields, but now, during the warm season, they are usually travelling to China to buy goods. Everyone wants to do business. This is how times have changed."

Gilgit, December 1994

### 2.2.3 Other professions

Another important source of income for Pashtun migrants were jobs linked to the colonial administration. Since this kind of work guaranteed a stable salary, it was highly popular with locals and outsiders alike. Most of these employment opportunities were to be found in Gilgit Town, the Agency's up-and-coming centre.

In his eyewitness account of the Hunza-Nager military campaign in 1891/92 the English journalist E.F. Knight (Knight, p. 273) mentions a group of Pashtuns, who earned their living as daily labourers working on the extension of the Kashmir-Gilgit route, an undertaking organized in order to facilitate the movement of soldiers and supplies. Knight describes them as outlaws, who had fled their homelands in fear of revenge for committed crimes. Later, during the actual military action they doubled as irregular fighting force. It is not excluded that some of these Pathan road builder-fighter-outlaws may have subsequently settled in Gilgit Town, or that their example could have inspired other fugitives to follow them into the area. At any rate, only fourteen years later B.E.M. Gurdon, the then British Political Agent in Gilgit, while referring to contracts given out by the local military engineer, was already speaking of "a good deal of money which is now earned by Baltis and Pathans" (quoted after Kreutzmann 1989, p. 186).

In fact, the practice of hiring Pashtun migrants as construction labour must have prevailed well into the 1920s. This is testified by the family history of *Sayed Rahman*, the owner of a China silk shop in Gilgit, whose paternal grandfather *Sayed Emtiyaz* had fled in the 1920s from Swat over Indus Kohistan into the Wazarat's territory. There he started his new professional life as a humble daily worker crushing rocks used for road surface and the building of houses. Later he managed to get better and more responsible assignments and over the years turned into a successful contractor for publicly financed constructions. With the money earned in this way he was able to settle his blood dues at home, acquire fallow land in the settlement of Chamurga (Gilgit District) and bring his family over from Swat. In the mid 1990s his descendents were living as businessmen in Gilgit, counting themselves among the town's most wealthy and respectable families.

The newly set up police force Pashto speakers seem to have joined from very early on; and obviously managed to make themselves disliked in comparatively short time. Hence, the already quoted B.E.M. Gurdon felt obliged to report to his superiors already in 1905 that: "Half of the policemen are Pathans who have been enlisted by the present *Wazir-i-Wazarat* [head of Kashmiri administration]. It is a great pity that these Pathans were ever allowed to obtain footing in Gilgit" (quoted after Kreutzmann 1989, p. 89, 94). However, Gurdon's rather critical remark seemed to have had little effect on local recruitment policies, as Pathan involvement into the Wazarat's law enforcement set-up was bound to continue until well into the 1930s. About this I learned from members of Pathan households in present day Sultanabad, a settlement formerly called Gujurdas, to the north of Gilgit Town. The men I spoke to were identifying themselves as descendents of two Pashtun friends, *Wilayat Khan* and *Mahabullah Khan*, who, according to a story told to me by the latter's grandson, had to run away from their home village in the Khyber Agency during the early 1930s, after being unjustly accused of a gruesome murder. Escaping the victim's relatives who were seeking revenge they fled via Srinagar to Gilgit where they soon found employment with the local police. Later, through the intercession of the British Agent's office, both friends, now trusted law enforcement officers, were given the opportunity to acquire newly reclaimed land in Gujurdas. There they settled just around Independence; at the time of my research their children and grandchildren were running shops in Sultanabad bazaar and acted as middlemen in the trade with Nager and Hunza.

## 2.3  Post-Partition period (after 1947): Showing strong presence

Soon after the Indian Subcontinent achieved its independence in 1947 the Gilgit Agency and Baltistan attached themselves to the newly created State of Pakistan. Since the territory of what are now called the Northern Areas was claimed by Delhi as being integral part of Kashmir and thus rightly belonging to the Indian Union, the Pakistani government made it its foremost priority to establish a firm hold on the region. Consequently, the local administration was brought under direct control of the decision makers in Karachi and significantly expanded over the coming years. Similarly, Pakistani military presence was established in central places like Gilgit Town, Chilas and Skardu, as well as in the border areas.

In order to guarantee a stable development in the region the Pakistani government embarked on a series of economical and social measures. First of all there was the urgent need to reinstate the transportation links to the lowlands, disrupted as a result of the Sub-continent's partition. The traditional north-south supply route leading over the Burzil Pass to Srinagar, which had been playing a major role during the colonial period, could no longer be used since it crossed into parts of Kashmir, now under Indian control. Pakistan therefore invested in developing an already existing trail over the Babusar Pass to Mansehra (NWFP) widening and

*Children in Jutial, Gilgit*

levelling it by the 1950s into a track also accessible for all-wheel drive vehicles. For the next 30 years, this technically challenging route, which even with pack animals could normally only be used during the snow-free season, was destined to remain the area's most important connection to the plains. Parallel to it, permanent air links, serving military as well as civilian purposes, were established between Gilgit and Peshawar and later also between Skardu and Rawalpindi.

During the decades following Independence sustained efforts were made to improve the network of roads and bridges within the region. Chief among these cost and labour intensive measures were the building of the Indus Valley Road, giving Baltistan a sustainable land link to Gilgit and to the lowlands, the gradual improvement of the Gilgit-Gupis road, and, the venture with the most far-reaching consequences, the construction of the Karakoram Highway.

Apart from expanding the administrative set-up and improving the road infrastructure, the Pakistani state also furthered the development of public health care and education. Thus, in the mid 1990s one could find hospitals in the main urban centres and dispensaries scattered throughout the rural areas. Besides this, a well-attended network of publicly financed primary and middle schools was reaching out until the remotest villages, setting a positive example for the rest of Pakistan.

### 2.3.1 Prior to the Karakoram Highway: A lead in trade and crafts

In the decades after the Northern Areas' accession to Pakistan the region's economy underwent a gradual shift of emphasis, in the result of which agriculture step by step receded to the background, whereas trade increased in importance, slowly but surely moving towards centre stage.

If one would have to identify the main beneficiaries of the first ten to fifteen years of this Post-Partition surge of commerce, Pashto-speaking migrants would be surely among them. There are at least two reasons for this. The first one is connected to the fact that, as illustrated above, already in colonial times Pashtun entrepreneurs had been exercising (at least partial) control over key market segments in Ghizar and Gilgit. The second one has to do with the political situation which occurred in the result of the partition of British-India and the ensuring war of its two successor states over Kashmir. This violent conflict was brought to an end with the establishment of a Line of Control (LOC) which cut right through the territory associated with the former Principality. Following this formal division into 'ours' and 'theirs' Hindu and Sikh businessmen related to what was now Kashmir's Indian controlled half found themselves compelled to leave the territory claimed by Pakistan. Like their Pashtun counterparts most of these 'Kashmiris', as they were habitually called by the local population, had been active in Gilgit Town, Gupis and Chilas over much of the colonial period. Now, their sudden collective departure created a commercial vacuum. This void was subsequently filled by Pathan merchants, as they were the only entrepreneurs remaining in the region, able and willing to mobilise the resources required for reviving the market. But taking over the customers of the Kashmiris as well as their abandoned shops and storage facilities was only half of the deal. Another advantage was, that the Pathan traders also continued to enjoy the transport monopoly over the Ghizar route, which after the LOC-induced interruption of the Gilgit-Srinagar connection had regained its role as the area's most important supply line. The combination of these factors allowed the Pashtun merchants to significantly enhance their position in the local bazaars, putting them – albeit only for a short period – into full control over the trade in the western part of the Northern Areas.[19]

In order to respond adequately to the situation, leading trader families like those of *Sarwar Khan* from Gupis/Gilgit and *Mohammad Daud* from Bassin/Gilgit had not only to increase the quantity of merchandise brought in from the outside, but also to reinforce the transport of goods via the Shandur Pass and their distribution in the area. All this required additional helping hands, whom the traders, at least for positions with financial responsibility, preferred to recruit from among their kinsmen, since local people were generally regarded as rather unreliable business partners. It is thus hardly surprising, that a number of older interviewees recalled for the years following Independence an increase of Pashto-speaking entrepreneurs from Bajaur and Dir operating in Ghizar, Gilgit and Chilas Districts.[20]

However, despite all the efforts made by the Ghizar merchants, in the long run increasing local demand could not be adequately sustained only by goods delivered through Chitral. The exploitation of this long, technically difficult route, whose vital passes were blocked by snow almost half of the year, resulted in regular delays. Besides this, high transportation costs reflected on the market prices. Hence, growing local requests for a faster supply of cheaper goods clearly favoured the shorter and, after its development in 1949, also technically superior connection over

---

19  In its eastern part, today's Skardu and Ganche Districts, expelled Kashmiri merchants were not replaced by Pashto-speaking traders. According to Dittmann (1997a, pp. 119-121) the reason for this was Baltistan's underdeveloped road connection to the rest of the country.

20  An official census from 1951 shows 665 Pashtuns living in the Gilgit Agency. Their distribution by the administrative units of that time was the following: Chilas 453, Gilgit 31, Punyal 6, Hunza 0, Nager 0, Ishkoman 27, Yasin 4, Kuh/Ghizar 144 (Government of Azad Kashmir, quoted after Kreutzmann 2005b, p. 8).

the Babusar Pass and via the Kaghan Valley. From the 1950s onwards this increasingly popular transport link, which allowed a more direct access to the main production centres of the lowlands, facilitated the influx of new outside trading competitors, mostly Hindko speakers originating from Hazara Subdivision and the adjoining Pakistan-administered Kashmir. But, at the same time it also opened the area to an increased arrival of Pashto speakers belonging to other places than Bajaur and Dir.[21]

Over the coming years many of these new arrivals managed to establish themselves in the bazaars of Chilas and Gilgit. In the latter Pashtun traders opened their shops primarily at three sites, all of them centrally located and close to the big suspension bridge: at Sadar Bazaar, Sabzi Mandi and, of course, at the time-honoured Kashmiri Bazaar. It was in this market, in a shop run by his younger brother, that I first spoke to *Muhammad Iqbal Khan*, a ca. 55-year-old cloth merchant from Chilas. Later, I continued my interview in his home town, where he owned one of the main garment shops. This is what *Muhammad Iqbal Khan* told me about the beginning of his business in the 1950s:

> "I live in Chilas since more then 30 years. My family originally hails from Attok [a town on the border between the NWFP and Punjab]. My father was also a merchant. He had a shop in Nowshera [a town east of Peshawar]. I was assisting him since I was a little boy. But my elder brother was going to take over my father's shop and so, if I wanted something on my own, I had to take my chances elsewhere.
>
> Then, my father got an order for sending cloth to the north, to Chilas; and I was put in charge of bringing the stuff there. At that time, a friend of mine had already mentioned Gilgit to me, so I had a vague idea where it was; somewhere in the mountains, close to Kashmir, this much I knew. But Chilas?! With this knowledge and with lots of fear in my heart, I started my first trip into

---

21   According to Sökefeld (1998b, p. 288) the majority of Pathans arriving to Gilgit in the years immediately after the opening of the Kaghan Route came from the village of Dodial close to Mansehra (Hazara Subdivision, NWFP).

*Mochis (cobblers) in the Main Bazaar of Chilas*

the unknown. In those days these places here were very far away, indeed. First, I went to Mansehra [centre of Hazara Subdivision], then with a mule caravan along the Kaghan Valley and over the still snow-covered Babusar Pass. As I said, I had only an eye on the merchandise during the transport. As for its sale, on arrival to Chilas I handed it over to a man from Muzaffarabad in Kashmir, who run a shop in the old bazaar. Despite all my apprehensions, all went well and we even got more orders. Thus, I repeated the trip two, three times.

Somehow, I started to like Chilas. In those days its bazaar was much smaller than now. Some of the shops here were owned by Pashtuns. Among them were *Nur Muhammad* from Peshawar – his son now owns the business just across the street – and *Ahmad Yusufzai* from Mardan – he died three years ago, and his general store is now run by a Swati from Mansehra. And, not to forget, *Dilawar*, a younger brother of the famous *Tuti Rahman* from Bajaur, who returned to the rest of his clan in Gilgit a couple of years ago. There were also traders and barbers from Hazara and a Mochi from Bajaur.

After observing the place for a while I decided to set up a general store here, too. I borrowed some money from my father and together with my younger brother *Yunus Khan* – it was in his shop in Gilgit that you and me first met – I rented a stall in the old bazaar. I handled sales and my brother took care of purchase and transport. Later, I brought in my cousin *Iqbal* and we were able to keep the business open even in winter. We rented a tiny house – only one room – and all three of us lived there for some time. The business was very good, especially in the beginning, when our shop was the most popular place for buying good, cheap cotton fabric in the whole bazaar. Then, with the profits accumulated over the first years, I bought some land, build my own house and got married. In the 1970s my brother moved to Gilgit, because the people there have more money. But, on the other hand, there are also constant problems with the local Shiites, which can make life in this town very dangerous, so I clearly prefer Chilas over it. Here everybody is of our faith and we Pashtuns are well respected."

Gilgit/Chilas, January-February 1995

In the years following *Muhammad Iqbal Khan's* arrival to the Northern Areas, the exceptionally strong position in which he still encountered the local Pashto-speaking trader community was slowly but surely subjected to a change. When in the beginning of the 1960s the British researcher John Staley surveyed the bazaars of Gilgit he counted 75 Pashtun and Hazara business holders active there. Representatives of other non-local groups, summed up by Staley under the names of 'Kashmiris' and 'Kashgharis', were only 41 in number (Staley 1966, pp. 249-250, quoted after Kreutzmann 1989, p. 187). Although this ratio clearly indicates that at that time Pashto speakers still constituted by-far the largest group of outsider entrepreneurs in town, the picture alters significantly, if we take into consideration the total amount of traders included into Staley's study. In this case Pashtun and Hazara entrepreneurs make up for no more than 20%, as the majority of the shops were now owned by local traders, Shina- and Burushaski speakers, who had begun to seize their share of the continuously expanding Gilgit market. With all likelihood a similar tendency will also have prevailed in Chilas. However, as we shall see further on, the Pashtun traders' loss of numerical advantage did not automatically go hand in hand with a decline of their economic supremacy. In fact, many more years were bound to pass before autochthonous traders would be able to compete with Pashtun merchants in business operations requiring high investment and systematic contacts to partners outside the Northern Areas.

Although during the 1950s the Pathan-controlled Chitral trade route must have lost much of its importance for the bazaars of Diamer and Gilgit Districts, as the bulk of imported merchandise now routinely arrived over the Babusar Pass, Pashtun trade leadership seemed to have remained unbroken in Ghizar, which continued to receive its goods first and foremost via the Shandur Pass. In addition to this, the position of the Pashto speakers active in Ghizar District was further strengthened by a decision of the local authorities to encourage outsiders to acquire reclaimed arable land.

A characteristic example for how this proactive settlement policy reflected on Pashtun migration can be seen in Taus, a village in the central part of Yasin Valley. There, in the autumn of 1994 I counted a total of nine Pathan households. Virtually all of the people I spoke to in this little colony of Pashto-speaking traders and craftsmen on the Roof of the World were descendents of Paracha settlers who came to the place during the 1950s. If the intention of the then administration had been to increase the commercial development of Yasin Valley by settling professional traders there, its efforts can be said to have met with a fair amount of success. For nearly 40 years humble Taus, with its busy, well supplied bazaar, was the undisputed market centre of the valley. Only in the second half of the 1980s its position was gradually taken over by nearby Yasin Village, the main settlement of the valley, to which at the time of my study also most of the Taus traders had shifted the bigger part of their business.

Other places in the Ghizar District with permanent Pashto-speaking trader households included the just mentioned Yasin Village, where the first Paracha settled as early as 1952, Imit and also Chatorkhand. In the mid 1990s Pathans were still holding key positions in the bazaars of all these places.

Another interesting episode in the Northern Areas' post-Partition Pashtun settlement history is the migration of a merchant family from Yarkand. Until well into the 20th century, this town which is situated in what is now the far west of China's Xinjiang Autonomous Region acted as a trading hub connecting East Turkistan with the markets of the surrounding countries. Over the years a number of outside merchants, among them Pathans engaged in organising and supervising large-scale commercial operations with Chitral and Afghanistan, had established themselves there. One of these entrepreneurs was a certain *Fazil Rahman Khan* who had arrived in East Turkistan from Bajaur sometimes in the second half of the 19th century. Both by blood and by business *Fazil Rahman Khan* was related to *Muhammad Kabari*, whose family had been engaged in the Karakoram trade since the early 1920s. In the mid 1950s, after the communist revolution in China, a number of people from East Turkistan, seeking protection from increasing economic and ideological oppression at home, fled across the border into Pakistan. Among these refugees were also members of the *Fazil Rahman Khan* family. With the support of the *Kabari* clan, part of which at that time was settled in Ghizar, they were soon able to re-start life and business; first in Taus and later also in Gilgit Town. At the time of my research *Fazil Rahman Khan's* descendants owned shops in Gupis and Gilgit. Besides this, they had managed to re-establish contact with the rest of their family in Yarkand, in partnership with whom they were now running a flourishing trade in Chinese silk.

Like in the Gilgit Agency also in Baltistan trade was negatively effected by the establishment of the Kashmir Line of Control. There it had interrupted the commercial supply routs, running through Srinagar and

Leh, now both under Indian supremacy.[22] But differently from the Agency, which, as we have seen, could still fall back on the Ghizar rout, in the case of Baltistan there was no other reliable land link with the Pakistani mainland readily available. Thus, for many years after Independence the systematic supply of the region with merchandise was heavily relying on flights operating between Skardu and Rawalpindi. This situation only changed in the early 1970s, when with the completion of the Indus Valley Road, a direct land route also suitable for the transport of goods by truck was finally set up. As was to be expected, this improved connection to the rest of Pakistan triggered the local market economy and encouraged the influx of outside traders. In the summer of 1976, three years after the Indus Valley Road's official opening, the Italian geographers Pierpaolo Faggi and Mario Ginestri carried out a survey of the network of market places in the upper Indus Valley (Faggi; Ginestri, p. 335). As for Baltistan their study registered the presence of outside traders only in the bazaars of Skardu Town, where besides five 'Kashmiris', two 'Turkis' and two 'Punjabis', the researchers also encountered three 'Pathans'. One of them might well have been the late *Mohammad Ismail Khan* whose son *Nizamuddin* I met during a visit to Skardu in October 1994. This is what he told me about how his family arrived to Baltistan:

> "My father was originally from Dir. He had left his home as a young man and then worked for some years as driver in Delhi and Lahore. After Partition, he went back to his father's house. But he could not find a decent job there for a long time. Also, the people in Dir could not understand his views. He had seen the world and his co-villagers didn't even know what an automobile was. One of his childhood friends ran a business in Gilgit. My father invested all his money in a joint transaction with him. He also accompanied the caravan to Gilgit in order to oversee the transport of his goods.

---

22  Before Independence the main bazaars of what are now Skardu and Ganche Districts were situated in Kargil and in Skardu Town. Contemporary sources describe the majority of traders there as 'Kashmiris', 'Panjabis' and 'Sikhs' (Faggi; Ginestri, p. 326).

When my father arrived there, he found the place to his liking. Almost immediately he got a job with a workshop as a jeep mechanic. He knew his profession well and people like him were much in demand there in those days. He made good money and was able to bring me and my mother over to live with him. In addition, he continued his partnership with his friend, who in the meantime had set up a shop in Kashmiri Bazaar. When the Skardu-Gilgit road got build, my father and I tried to develop a transport service between Gilgit and Skardu. We only had two jeeps and the drive was very dangerous. Spending time in Skardu, we saw that the cotton fabric available in the market was either of poor quality or far too expensive. And there was no good choice, unlike in Gilgit. Actually, most supplies came from Rawalpindi by air. Some people would make special shopping trips to there or to Gilgit to buy clothes for weddings or festive occasions. This is when my father decided to set up a shop in Skardu. In the beginning, we rented a tiny stall in the Old Bazaar, but around 20 years ago we opened this shop here in Amidgar Bazaar.

In 1985, my father returned to Gilgit, but my elder brother and I stayed on. We built ourselves a house nearby, where we now live with our families. I am linked by marriage to a Pashtun trader family in Gilgit. My brother has taken his wife from among our clan in Dir. There are many Pashtuns in Skardu now.[23] They trade mostly in fabric and in Chinese goods. Others are in the recycling business, run a tea stall or work as cobblers, just like the one across the street. In fact, even the owner of the cinema hall belongs to a family originally from Bajaur."

Skardu, October 1994

Side-by-side with the settled merchants, and mostly depending on them for their supplies, itinerant traders – similar to those already described for

---

[23] According to Dittmann (1997a, p. 122) in the mid 1990s the majority of traders in Skardu who did not originate from Baltistan were Pathans from the NWFP.

the colonial period – continued to be active throughout the region. As a typical representative of such mobile entrepreneurs we can take the late *Rezaq Khan*, who had started his career as a shop assistant in Gilgit and subsequently established his own business, selling goods in the settlements of the nearby valleys. His son *Abdul Qayyum*, a ca. 45-year-old businessman from Gilgit, who himself had been living for many years in Spain, working as an itinerant jewellery maker, told me the following about his father:

> "My father's origins are in Bajaur. His parents had died early and since he felt unwanted in his uncle's family he left his village and went to Peshawar in search of a living. He worked there for a couple of years as a day labourer. Once he killed a man in a fight and, afraid that the slain man's friends would seek revenge, he fled to Mansehra. From there, he came about 40 years ago as a caravan helper to Gilgit. Here he worked first as a porter. Later, *Payanda Khan*, the owner of the General Store in Raja Bazaar, employed him as one of his assistants.

*Abdul Qayyum and his eldest son*

In the service of *Payanda Khan* my father travelled to the surrounding valleys and sold goods there. In the course of his travels he realized that there was good money in this trade, as whatever outside goods the farmers were in need of, they had to bring them from Gilgit with great difficulty. There really weren't many itinerant traders in those days, and permanent shops could be found only in the large settlements. So my father decided to start his own business. He had already married by then. My mother belongs to a family of Kashmiri origin settled in Pari Bangla, a village on the way to Jaglot. His parents-in-law helped my father with the little money they had and from a Pashtun friend, who owned a small shop in the bazaar, he acquired goods on a commission basis: mainly salt, sugar and tea, but also some knickknacks like needles, buttons, brooches and pocket mirrors. All this he carried in a wicker basket to the villages, where he sold the things for a good profit. In summer he was a trader in the valleys and in the winter he mended shoes in Gilgit's Raja Bazaar, a craft he had learned during his stay in Peshawar.

We children, my brothers and I, helped him ever since we learned to walk. I often accompanied him on his trips to Bagrot [a valley to the east of Gilgit], which was our favourite place. We would set off together from our home, he with his basket and I with a bundle on my back. Sometimes my father would stop on the way in Danyor and pick up an order of iron goods made by the local blacksmith: sickles, knives and other things that the farmers had asked for in earlier visits. From Danyor we used to head for Bagrot, always on foot and constantly hungry, with our heavy loads. But it was a wonderful time, especially in the valley itself where everyone knew my father. The men called him by his name – *Rezaq Khan*. The women would come out of their houses to greet us; the children would shout 'Pathan! Pathan!'. My father also accepted wool and goat hair as payment, because very few villagers had any money. We would sleep in the open, sometimes also in the houses of friends or in the village mosque. As you know, Bagrot is a Shiite place, but no one seemed to mind the fact that my father was a Sunnite. The people would give us mulberries and apricots, bread and butter. In Bagrot we were never hungry. And everybody was very kind to us. After all, they needed my father's goods. In later years he mainly supplied Bagrot, travelling there thrice or four times during the snow-free season. Other small traders went to Shinaaki [here: region in the lower Hunza/Nager Valley], Chalt [a valley north of Gilgit] and Punyal.

Two years ago I went back to Bagrot after a very long time. In the village of Datuchi an old man asked me: 'Aren't you the son of *Rezaq Khan*?' My father died a long time ago but his name still lives on in Bagrot. You can imagine how happy I was to hear him remembered by the people."

Gilgit, January-March 1995

## 2.3.2 With the Karakoram Highway: Reaping the economic benefits

When after more than a decade construction time the Karakoram Highway (KKH) was finally officially opened in 1978, the sheer scale of the work accomplished must have given an indication of the far-reaching changes its exploitation would bring about. Built with the participation of hundreds of Chinese workers and engineers this two lane, black top road traverses the entire Karakoram region, starting from its southern limits up to its northern geological border with the Pamirs. Conceived as a strategic link with China, the KKH, which in many places on its way had to be blasted through massive walls of rock, can be used the whole year around by motorised transport, including trucks, busses and other heavy vehicles. It thus guarantees an unprecedented quick and reliable connection between the high mountain country and the industrial centres of Pakistan. And, besides this, by crossing the country's state border at the Khunjarab Pass it also assures an easy access to the emerging markets of China and Central Asia.

As was to be expected, the exploitation of such a highly efficient thoroughfare facilitated not only the movement of people and goods, but also the exchange of concepts and ideas. The ensuing radical exposure to outside influences stimulated a thorough shake-up of the entire region's economic and social setting, catapulting the Northern Areas from centuries of provincial drowsiness straight into modern times.[24]

The place most strongly affected by all these changes was certainly Gilgit. In the mid 1990s the town experienced an enormous economic boom, exemplified by an almost explosive expansion of its bazaar structures and the constant enlargement in the variety of goods offered in their shops. Gilgit's extraordinary development was doubtlessly connected to the fact that by that time the town had not only reaffirmed and strengthened its traditional position as the area's main trading centre, but also introduced itself as the Karakoram's focal point for the turnover of goods and services from China.[25]

However, it was not only Gilgit and the other urban centres, which by the time of my research had benefited from the recent infrastructural improvements. The development had clearly reached out also to the rural areas. So, on a number of places where main roads, like the KKH or the Indus Valley Road were joined by secondary ones, previously existing bazaar structures had significantly grown in size or completely new trading areas had sprung up.[26] These road markets normally served a dual purpose. On the one hand they were resting places for transiting passengers and drivers, on the other they acted as supply nodes for the adjoining villages and side valleys. In the mid 1990s typical examples of such freshly developed trade and service areas were to be found in Jaglot

---

24 For a detailed discussion of the impact of road construction on mountain societies on the example of the KKH and the Northern Areas see Allan 1989; Kreutzmann 1991.

25 With approximately 1.500 shops in its bazaars Gilgit was in 1995 the by far largest trading place in the Northern Areas (Dittmann 1998, p. 53).

26 Just to give an impression of the speed of the overall development: Dittmann (1997b, p. 119) estimated that while in the bazaars of central places like Gilgit and Skardu the number of shops and workshops was redoubling approximately every nine years, some commercial sub-centres would go through the same process in just the half of this time.

*Shina speakers waiting for the bus in Jaglot (Gilgit District)*

(KKH, west of Gilgit), opposite Rondu (Indus Valley Road, west of Skardu), in Aliabad (KKH, central Hunza), in Sost (KKH, last resting place before the Pakistani-Chinese border) and, arguably the largest of them all, on both sides of the KKH just below Chilas.

### 2.3.2.1 Traders and smugglers

Considering their sharp sense for profitable business, it seems only natural that Pashtun entrepreneurs were among the first to exploit the commercial opportunities created in the wake of the new infrastructural opening. Over the 1980s and '90s many of the ones who had already settled in the area were able to consolidate their position or to expand their business activities to new and unprecedented spheres. The same decades also saw an unparalleled rise in new Pathan arrivals. In fact, by the mid 1990s seasonal Pashto-speaking migrants had clearly outnumbered their permanent counterparts.

Most of these recent migrants took up business in the bazaars of the urban centres. Particularly in Gilgit, there were so many Pathan entrepreneurs that walking through certain commercial parts of the town a casual visitor would assume to be somewhere in Swat or Dir, rather than in a traditionally non-Pashto-speaking place. The shops which immediately caught ones eye in the urban markets belonged to the Pathan fruit and vegetable merchants, who, entirely absent from pre-KKH statistics, had by the 1990s managed to established themselves as an integral part of the Northern Areas' bazaar structure. In Gilgit the vegetable retailers were mostly concentrated in Cinema Bazaar and in Sabzi Mandi, whereas the wholesalers had put up shop in the upper part of Airport Bazaar. In addition to them, one could also encounter many mobile vegetable vendors who in search of interested customers were manoeuvring their flat-board push-carts along the town's side roads and into the residential areas. Most of the people engaged in the fruit and vegetable business had come from the Pashto-speaking lower Swat region, the fertile fields and gardens of which also furnished the bulk of the urban centres' fresh supplies. Even if an increasing amount of vegetables on sale was being produced locally and a number of related stalls were owned by members of autochthonous groups, it was evident that the vegetable retail trade in Gilgit, Skardu and Chilas was dominated by Pashto speakers; and the wholesale section fully controlled by them.

As in pre-KKH times, descendents of the Ghizar merchants, who counted themselves among the most affluent men in town, as well as Pathan traders from Hazara were still selling the best quality fabric in Gilgit bazaar. Their shops, complemented by numerous stalls belonging to freshly arrived compatriots, could mainly be found in Kashmiri and Sadar Bazaar. Similarly to their predecessors cloth merchants continued to procure their wares mostly from the Pakistani lowland but, ever since the opening of the border, more and more merchandise, especially silk, was now also coming in from China.

While the majority of shops operated by Pashtun entrepreneurs in Gilgit were part of already well established commercial clusters like Kashmiri, Raja, Momin and Airport Bazaar, a significant number of them could also be located in new sections, like for example in the freshly raised NLI Market. Within months of its inauguration in spring 1995 this vast commercial space – situated in the very centre of the town, on a place once occupied by the barracks of the Northern Light Infantry, the area's defence force – had developed into Gilgit's most important location for the purchase of all kinds of top-price-range merchandise. Parallel to this, it had also turned into the bazaar with the probably highest concentration of Pashto-speaking traders in the Northern Areas.[27] At the time of my research that market was mostly frequented by clients from the Pakistani lowlands, who were taking advantage of the Northern Areas' comparatively lower prices on imported goods. Competing for the costumers' attention where representatives of old-established merchant families – many of them with secondary shops elsewhere in town – side by side with recently arrived traders, who had put all their financial resources into the business, counting on a safe and fast return.

The rich assortment of luxury goods available in most of their shops as well as the required rent deposit of up to 400 thousand Pakistani Rupees (at that time about $ 10,000) clearly demonstrated not only the Pathan traders' business acumen and willingness to take risks, but also their vast investment capacity. Apart from high value cotton fabric and ready-made garments, NLI Market Pashto-speakers primarily dealt with wares from China such as silk, blankets and porcelain as well as expensive electrical and electronic devices.

Smaller shops usually received sporadic supplies from casual dealers, who purchased goods in China at their own risk and resold them on return to the Northern Areas. Well-established businessmen, who often were linked to traders in the lowlands, normally did not rely on freelance middlemen, but employed their own wholesale purchasers, usually close relatives entitled to a business partner's share in the turnover of the merchandise. Each spring, as soon as the Khunjarab Pass was snow-free and the border re-opened, a great number of these purchasers set off toward China, sometimes travelling as far as Shanghai and Hong Kong in search

---

27  Out of 111 NLI Market shops counted by Dittmann (1998, p. 73) in Septembers 1995, 68 were run by merchants speaking Pashto and/or originating from the NWFP.

of profitable deals. *Abdullah Khan*, whose family business was also represented in Peshawar and Dir, related to me the following about his last business trip:

> "My brother and I own two shops in Gilgit, this one here in Medina Market and a brand new one in NLI Market. My father has a shop at Peshawar's Sadar Bazaar. Five years ago we started buying goods in China, supplying our father's shop. We always reloaded our things in Gilgit and gradually realized that the city was good for serious business. First, because of the proximity of the border, so one can cut on transportation rates and offer the goods here cheaper than in down country. And second, because shop rents here are just about half of what they would be in Peshawar. And there are, of course, the customers: In the summers many Punjabis come to Gilgit to combine a family holiday in the mountains with a shopping trip. Others visit the town the whole year around, just for business, to buy Chinese goods on wholesale basis, since they are duty free here. This very shop was the first we opened, and because it was doing so well, we recently took another one at NLI Market. This NLI place is still new and the price for a shop there is much higher than elsewhere in town, but, as a saying goes, one has to invest into the future.
>
> My brother is in charge of the affairs here in Gilgit and I travel to China each year to buy goods. I am mostly interested in cassette recorders, walkmans, radios and similar electronic devices. We can sell them directly in our shops and the turnover is really good since these things are much cheaper than the Japanese brands that my father is getting through the Afghanistan trade.[28] I also buy fertilizer and silk fabric and I even brought back five moun-

---

28  The narrator is referring to the so called 're-export business', in which goods arriving in Pakistan from abroad (mainly by sea to Karachi) were officially declared as imports for Afghanistan, but than sold in the Tribal Areas and illegally returned to the Pakistani mainland, where they could be offered for a more competitive price, as they had not been subjected to import duty.

tain bikes last year. I usually travel by bus to Urumchi [capital of Xinjiang Region]. Earlier Kashghar [a city in Xinjiang, half way between the Pakistani border and Urumchi] also used to be a good place for trade but now there are too many of our businessmen there and the prices have risen.

Last summer, I first went to Urumchi, where I placed a large order for fertilizer. We usually sell it through my uncle's shop in Dir. But the supplier made me wait too long, so I decided to go further to the east of the country. I wanted to explore the market for electronic goods which were said to be cheaper there than in Xinjiang. Finally, I took a train to Shanghai. It was my first visit to this huge city but I was with some friends from Peshawar who knew the place, as they were doing this journey not for the first time. The cassette recorders were really cheaper in Shanghai, but I could not find a good transport opportunity and I anyway had to return to the fertilizer supplier in Urumchi. So, I bought Japanese silk instead, which I could take with me on the train in boxes. The whole Shanghai adventure took me almost one month, but back in Xinjiang I still had to wait two more weeks for the fertilizer. In the middle of August I returned to Pakistan with three trucks. Since we are not permanent residents of the Northern Areas we have no import license. But I know some people in the customs department in Sost. Usually I pay them between three and five Lakhs [300-500 thousand Pakistani Rupees] per load and they take care of everything. After crossing the border we reloaded our goods on Pakistani vehicles. Normally my brother sends drivers to wait for me, but Sost has a busy bazaar, so, whenever the need arises, I can also simply hire an additional lorry.

Going with goods from Sost to down country, one has to bring them across the many check-points on the way. Police, rangers, and customs – everyone wants to make some money from us traders. They simply block the road and demand a payment. Sometimes it costs a lot and sometimes they are satisfied with a couple of hundreds. Each time I think I know all the posts and each time new ones are emerging. They are no better than thieves and highway robbers. These kinds of things could never have happened under General Zia [Military ruler of Pakistan, 1977 to 1988]. The cash hand-outs continue all the way to Peshawar and one is relieved of a whole lot of money. This is why smaller consignments or goods which do not have to be dispatched immediately I normally first bring to Gilgit. From here they are then sent further through private runner or a transport company. In this way one can avoid some of the extra payments.

Normally, between June and the closing of the border in November I manage to make two trips to China. The people there are not very welcoming but business is good and I know already many other business travellers whom I meet each time in the hotel or on the bus. In fact, a Pashtun from Swat who has married a local woman recently even set up a street restaurant in Kashghar, where we can eat our food and drink our tea. These are the things which make life in foreign lands more bearable."

Gilgit, May 1995

As is evident from *Abdullah Khan's* recollections, besides licensed, i.e. legal importation, there existed also other, less official ways to bring goods from China over the Khunjarab Pass into Pakistan. In fact, during the time of my research border traffic in contraband seemed to have been so widespread that people actively involved in it were, as we have seen in the aforementioned example, not hesitant or embarrassed to speak about it even with a foreigner. Actually, the smuggling procedure applied was extremely simple – one trader described it as the "pay and go approach" – with the quantity of goods involved ranging from a bundle taken as hand luggage into the public border bus up to several tons loaded onto privately rented lorries.

Although representatives of all ethnic groups present in the Northern

Areas participated in and profited from that kind of unauthorized border trade, Pashtun entrepreneurs were often singled out for their – as one of my local interviewees pointedly called it – "shameless abuse of a well-functioning system". Among other excesses, those interviewed listed Pathan involvement in illegal cross-border business connected with drugs, antiques and protected animal species. Of course, these kinds of general allegations are never easy to prove. However, they seemed not to be completely unfounded, as is evident from the following story told by *Naunihal*, Burushaski speaker from Gilgit, which is devoted to an encounter with Pashtun falcon smugglers in Kashghar:

> "It happened around three years ago. At that time I used to work as the representative of Walji's Travel Agency in Kashghar. Once, when I sat in my bureau in Chini Bagh Hotel, a Chinese customs official acquainted to me called me up and asked me to see him in his office. There he told me that his colleagues at the Chinese-Pakistani border in Tashkurghan had caught five Pathans, citizens of Pakistan, with living falcons in their luggage. Smuggling falcons is a very profitable business, entirely controlled by traders from Peshawar, who are making a fortune out of it. These beautiful birds are in high demand, mainly in Saudi Arabia and the Emirates. Every little Sheikh there is desperate to have his own hunting falcon but since you can't find them anymore in the desert, they have to be imported. As falcons are a rare and protected species, it is not always easy to acquire one, but the Sheikhs are ready to pay any amount of money for it. And, as we say, where there is a buyer, there is also a Pathan.
>
> One area where one can still encounter many falcons is the mountains of Xinjiang, right here over the border in China. So, the rich Arabs, through their middlemen, contact specialists in Peshawar, whose job it is to find the birds and bring them into Pakistan. The falcon business as such can be divided into three stages: trapping, transport and sale. The Pathans are responsible for the transport and the sale, while trapping is taken care of by

the locals. Although, according to Chinese law, catching these birds is an illegal act, the prospective cash acts as a strong incentive, so there is no shortage of Kashgharis giving in to the temptation. Once a falcon is in the net, it is passed on to the smugglers. These are professional gangs, who often have their own veterinarian with them since the birds are extremely sensitive, the journey is long and no one wants to run any risks in view of the large sums of money involved. So, the Pathans take over the bird, give it a sedative, stitch its eyes shut, hide it in their luggage and off they go to the border. The birds fall under a strict export ban in China and the official penalty for falcon smuggling is draconian. In our case, the Chinese authorities had apparently caught one of these gangs – just imagine, these clever Pathans were said to have had hidden the drugged birds in empty thermos flasks – and wanted to put its members on public trial as a deterrent for other poachers.

The trial took place in the city court of Kashghar, where apart from men and women in all kinds of uniforms there was also a sizable public presence, including a team from the Chinese Television. I was the representative of Pakistan, so to say, invited to give to the whole performance the required international touch. The authorities had even provided for a Urdu-Chinese interpreter, who took pains to translate every word for me. The trial did not last long. The public prosecutor and the defence thundered patriotic speeches; the accused admitted their guilt and an angry judge pronounced sentences of five to seven years. The convicted enemies of the state looked quite crestfallen. I started to wonder about the prospects of these men, sentenced to so many years, to be spent in one of these notorious Chinese labour camps.

I don't like Pathans, and certainly I did not like these smugglers who gave our country a bad name while earning a lot of money for themselves. But, after all, they were my fellow citizens and I somehow felt sorry for them. The judge had ruled that they were to start serving their sentence immediately, so I went up to the group and asked whether I could get them a few things from home. 'What things, man?' they shouted, 'We can get them ourselves, once we are back. But who is going to reimburse all the money that we had to pay these sons of bitches for our freedom? And they even took the birds away!' A week later, by the time an official feature about the trial was aired on Chinese Television, our Pathan friends were already safe and sound back in Peshawar and I bet it will not be the last time that I see them around."

Gilgit, May 1995

Besides well-established Pathan merchants and professional Pathan smugglers, whose activities were not always easily distinguishable, and who were normally operating with hefty investments, under high risks and on regional/supra-regional level, the Northern Areas also continued to attract many small-scale businessmen. But, in contrast to their more illustrious brethren, the majority of them acted only on a purely local basis and with many fewer assets at their disposal. Probably the most characteristic representatives of this brand of entrepreneurs were the mobile traders, highly popular with the residents of the rural areas and already well-known to us from pre-KKH times.

In the mid 1990s it wasn't easy to find a village of any significance not periodically visited by travelling Pashto-speaking businessmen.[29] The choice of goods traded by them reflected their and their clients' limited financial possibilities. Thus, threads, needles, buttons, simple cosmetics, ball point pens, cooking utensils, knives as well as toys and school material for children were among the most common articles on offer. Other, more specialised, entrepreneurs dealt in inexpensive shoes and cotton cloth or bought dried fruits, mushrooms, herbs, nuts, bones, goat hair,

---

29 The only prominent exception to this was ironically Bagrot, the valley so fondly remembered by *Abdul Qayyum*, son of *Rezaq Khan*, while recalling his father's business travels in the 1960s. At the time of my research Bagrot was carefully avoided by travelling Pathan traders, as they feared acts of hostility from its Shiite inhabitants, whom they suspected of harbouring strong anti-Sunnite sentiments.

*Family in Bagrot Valley*

wool, hides and recyclable material, such as plastic, empty tins and paper. Most of these goods were then brought to central collection points in the bazaars of Gilgit, Chilas and Skardu and from there either resold or further dispatched to the South. As can be seen from this listing, items dealt with were still very much the same as in the 1960s, or during the colonial period, for that matter. What had changed though, was the business environment. While petty traders like *Rezaq Khan* used to move around on foot, carrying the merchandise on offer on their own back or, at best, on a mule, their modern counterparts toured the villages more or less comfortably in public minibuses or collective jeep taxis.

No doubt, these new transportation facilities had made the toil of the modern mobile traders much easier, but they also stimulated the travel of their potential customers to central bazaar places, where they could market their products themselves and purchase the things they needed out of a larger selection and for a more competitive price. Besides this, over the previous decades basic shops run by local businessmen – often retired army personal or state pensioners – had appeared in many of the settlements. The goods to be found on their shelves normally included the ones offered by the travelling entrepreneurs and most of their owners also acted as middlemen for dried fruits and local forest products. As a result, Pathan mobile traders, although still very active in the region, were facing an increasingly stiff competition, which in consequence, one may assume, could lead to a gradual disappearance of their time-honoured profession.

What will probably remain unchallenged, though, is the Pashto speakers' leading role in the purchase and resale of bones, hides and recyclable industrial material. First of all, few members of autochthonous ethno-linguistic groups would consider engaging in this trade, as dealing with such kind of products is traditionally regarded as polluting and degrading. And second, and, maybe even more important, in the mid 1990s Pashtuns were still the only ones, who entertained professional contacts to tanneries and workshops in the plains, specialising on the processing of these items.

### 2.3.2.2 CRAFTSMEN

Besides a significant influx of new traders, the KKH also stimulated an increased arrival of craftsmen. Most noticeable among them were the cobblers. In their places of origin, mostly Bajaur and Dir, many of them belonged to families, traditionally engaged in the tanning of hides and the processing of leather.

As early as 1964 Staley counted twelve of these leatherworkers in the bazaars of Gilgit Town, dating their arrival back to the previous years (Staley 1966, p. 96, quoted after Kreutzmann 1989, p. 187). Moreover, judging from the reminiscences of *Sarwar Khan* and childhood memories of other elderly interviewees, Pathan Mochis seem to have been present (at least) in Gupis and Gilgit already in pre-Independence times.

In the mid 1990s these specialized craftsmen could be encountered all over the Northern Areas. Almost each bazaar had at least one tiny spot or shaky wooden booth where a tireless cobbler was bestowing new life on the torn leather shoes and plastic sandals of his patiently waiting cus-

*Tailors in their workshop in Chilas*

tomers. The rent for the cobbler's place was low, the tools of his trade simple and inexpensive, and the amount of things to be mended endless. Besides this, professional competition was limited to the artisan's compatriots, as most members of autochthonous groups regarded his occupation as much below their status. Under these favourable circumstances it seems only natural that cobblers were by far the largest Pashto-speaking group of craftsmen in the Northern Areas.

Apart from the Mochis who were working the year round on a fixed spot, there were others who during the warm season would pay visits to costumers in far flung villages. Like the travelling traders, mobile leather-workers had their very personal, well-established business routes, on which they did not tolerate any contenders. And also similar to them, cobblers hardly ever shifted their permanent residence to the Northern Areas, as, according to the statement of one of my Mochi interviewees "even working day and night would never bring enough money to support wife and children in this strange and unwelcoming place".

Other typical Pashto-speaking craftsmen encountered in the Northern

Areas were tailors and barbers. The first usually laboured in workshops in groups of three to seven people, often related to each other by family ties and/or originating from the same village. These Pashtun-run tailor shops, which in the mid 1990s were limited to the urban centres, had an excellent standing as their employees were reputed to display professional skills not equalled by the average local craftsman. The professionalism of the Pashtun tailors may have been connected to the fact, that many of them had previously been working in similar facilities in Peshawar or Swat and some of them had even gained experience in the country's large sewing factories. At least in Gilgit and Chilas owners of the more busy workshops did not object to instructing apprentices belonging to other ethno-linguistic groups. Hence, it was not unusual to encounter a local tailor master with a rudimentary knowledge of Pashto, who had learned his craft in one of the prestigious Pathan ateliers. Almost all of the Pashto-speaking tailors were temporary migrants, a circumstance which made itself particularly felt around major religious holidays when the best workshops in town remained closed for weeks on end, as everybody was away on home leave.

Similar to tailors, also most of the barbers used to come and work in the Northern Areas on a purely temporary basis. Barber shops, the bigger ones often doubling as public baths, could be found in all larger bazaars of the region. Apart from Pashtuns, the barber's trade was also regularly exercised by Hindko speakers, originating from Pakistan-administered Kashmir or from Hazara. It was interesting to observe, that while most members of autochthonous groups harboured a readily and strongly expressed aversion to everything connected with the barber's profession, their dislike obviously did not include the hair cutter's services as such. In fact, judging by the existence of an impressive number of trendy and extremely well-patronized salons, visiting the hairdresser's seemed to be the favourite local pastime. Connected to this passion, which was shared by young men from among all ethnic and religious backgrounds, one may recall an anecdote circulating in Gilgit during the mid 1990s. According to it, after the sectarian unrest of 1988 local fashion-conscious Shiite radicals were raising funds within their community in order to attract co-religionist hairdressers from Parachinar — a Shiite-majority town in the Kurram Tribal Agency — since they felt increasingly uncomfortable under the sharp razor blades of Sunnite barbers. Whether true or simply well invented, the story was echoed by the existence of a couple of barbershops in Gilgit and Danyor which were operated by recently arrived Shiite Pathans.

At the same time, Pashto-speaking barbers from Hazara were allegedly the first Sunnites who had succeeded in establishing themselves in the bazaar of Ismaili-dominated Karimabad (Hunza). *Sayed Akbar Khan*, the owner of the local hairdresser salon, related to me how he and his brother had arrived there:

> "I am from Abbottabad. My wife and my parents live there. We are affiliated to the Swatis and Pashto is our mother tongue. I have learnt the barber's craft from my father, and he from his father; in fact, it is the hereditary profession of our family. Already as a young boy I used to help out in my father's salon. Later on I set out to practice my trade in other places. First I went to Karachi, where I was employed with an experienced master in Pathan Town. It was a good time, and I made a decent amount of money, but then the city became restless. There was constant trouble between Pathans and Muhajirs [Urdu-speaking group in Karachi]. Although I personally did not have anything to do with these disturbances, it was still dangerous to speak Pashto or even to look like a Pathan. They beat up a friend of mine, another was arrested by the police for no reason and had to pay a hefty sum to bail himself out. I realized that there was no future for me in that town, so I left for Peshawar. There, I set up a small open stall in Cinema Bazaar, but my earnings were meagre and I could not rise enough money to rent a larger and better situated shop to which more customers would come. So, I went back to Abbottabad where I spoke to my father and than to my younger brother. We decided to set up a salon in Gilgit, because we had heard from a relative that there barbers were in de-

mand and shop rents low. Our father gave us money and we went to Gilgit. This was about five years ago.

We reached Gilgit just after the 1988 clashes. At that time many people there regarded Pashtuns as trouble makers. So we did not start anything, but went on to Gakuch [administrative centre of Ghizar District]. Initially we planned to return to Gilgit once the situation improved, but business in Gakuch, where we had installed ourselves in the main bazaar, was so good that we stayed on for two years. We employed an assistant and worked in turns; sometimes my brother was at home in Abbottabad and sometimes it was me.

Later on, a local Ismaili told us that barbers were needed in Aliabad, Hunza. This village is located on the road to China and all the buses stop there. This means lots of through traffic, plenty of shops and, subsequently, many customers. We ran a salon in Aliabad for another two years. There we often received customers from Karimabad [central settlement of Hunza Valley] who came all the way down just to get a shave in our shop. Meanwhile, two other barbers had set up shop in Aliabad, both from Hazara like us, but Hindko-speakers. Friends from Karimabad invited us to start business in their local bazaar. Initially, I wasn't interested at all, because every one knows how strange these Ismailis are and how little respect they have in their hearts for us Sunnites. Later, however, my younger brother argued strongly for the move: 'Please understand, that we would be the only barbers in the whole bazaar. The entire village would come to us and they have so much money'. That's how he spoke to me. And since one of their leaders promised to lease a place to us and to help, in case there were any problems, I finally agreed. Now we are here for more than a year and I have not regretted this move even for a minute."

Karimabad, May 1995

### 2.3.2.3 OTHER PROFESSIONS

One of the most characteristic indications of the area's fast economic development in the decades following the opening of the KKH was a sharp increase in privately financed construction activities. During the time of my research innumerable busy building sites for new hotels, so called 'shopping plazas' – usually nothing else than the accumulation of garage-like concrete structures along a sidewalk or around a small central square – and other commercial installations were to be found in the urban centres as well as in smaller centrally located places like Gupis, Gakuch, Yasin Village and Aliabad. While the people working at these sites could belong to any of the region's ethno-linguistic groups, there was a tendency for a certain origin-related division of labour. Hence, speakers of local languages and people from Kohistan normally functioned as engineers, contractors, masons and handymen, while Pashtuns mainly specialised in working with concrete. All Pashtun construction workers interviewed by me were temporary migrants. Usually they cooperated with a particular contractor, who not only handed them their pay and guaranteed their free lodging – all over Pakistan construction workers used to sleep in the unfinished building – but also took them along to a new site, once the old assignment was completed. Most of the specialists in concrete construction had previously been working with other contractors in the NWFP or in Punjab, and had shifted to the Northern Areas in search of better conditions. However, nobody I spoke to expressed any liking for the present place of work, as the new wage was generally lower than one had expected and the living conditions dictated by the cooler mountain climate much harder than in the Pakistani lowlands.

Equally prominent in the bazaars of Gilgit and Chilas were the Pashto-speaking porters. In fact, they were virtually impossible to go unnoticed, as by manoeuvring their heavily loaded, two-wheeled flat-board pushcarts through the market crowds they significantly contributed to the urban centres' general traffic chaos. All the porters made their living through day-to-day assignments received from the surrounding traders and transport companies. There was certainly no lack of work, but the

*Tea shop owner in Gilgit's Airport Bazaar*

money earned with their heavy labour was so little that none of the men I spoke to would even think about making the current place of his work his permanent home.

Another business, well-liked by Pashto-speakers, was the running of so called 'hotels', a term under which local parlance subsumed all kinds of inns, basic restaurants and tea stalls. Already during the early 1960s Staley counted as many as 23 such establishments in the bazaars of Gilgit, not specifying, however, which ethnic groups their respective owners belonged to (Staley 1966, p. 251, quoted after Kreutzmann 1989, p. 186).

A tremendous boost to the hotel business was given by the opening of the KKH, which brought about the arrival of hitherto unseen numbers of seasonal workers, traders and tourists all in need of shelter, food and tea. While the places catering to the needs of foreigners and (other) well-off customers were almost exclusively operated by autochthonous entrepreneurs, Pashto speakers had taken charge of the hospitality sector's more basic side. And they did it with a fair amount of success. Just to give a casual impression: In summer 1995 I found 17 hotels in the lower section of Gilgit's Airport Bazaar, eleven of which belonged to Pathan owners. In autumn 1994, Skardu's New Bazaar Road had a total of eight food stalls, half of them manned mainly by Pashto-speaking personnel. This much about the proportions in the urban centres. As for the newly established road-side bazaars, there were some of them, like the market in Sazin, the one in Sost, or the long-winding trade area below Chilas, where almost all basic eateries rested in Pathan hands.

It was interesting to observe, that most of these Pathan-run small enterprises, which often counted not more than a manager-cook and a serving boy, were operated by temporary migrants from Swat and Mardan, usually members of one extended family or hailing from the same village. From discussions with them it appeared that setting up a hotel was a concept popular with prospective investors and employees alike. The former found it attractive because the initial financial input could be kept at a minimum, which was due to the fact that the premises were normally not bought, but rented and then fitted out with only the most simple furniture and equipment. For the latter it was suitable, as – except for cooking – there were no special professional skills required: tea making, serving and cleaning could be quickly picked up during the first days of duty. Besides this, all interviewees cherished the idea that there were no communication barriers between them and their customers, since most of the migrant workers, traders and truck drivers frequenting these places were Pashto speakers anyway. One remained among one's own people, in a sense.

Many hotels employed children and youths as helpers. Grateful for a chance not to go hungry and, eventually, to earn even enough money to support their families back home, these boys frequently performed heavy and underpaid work. The 17-year-old *Dilraj*, a temporary migrant in Gilgit, told me the following about his career as a kitchen hand:

> "My family lives in Mardan. My father is a poor farmer and I have eight brothers and sisters. When I was six years old my elder brother *Kamran* took up a job in Gilgit. He was 15 years old at that time. My uncle *Mahbub* worked as a waiter in 'Vershigroom

Hotel' in Airport Bazaar. The manager of the hotel at that time was from our village and since they needed more service boys, my uncle brought my brother in. Two years later, my parents sent me to *Kamran* so he could teach me and I could live with him. In the beginning I used to wipe the tables and bring the tea. Later on, I was also allowed to serve the food.

In the meantime my brother had become a baker in 'Pathan Hotel', the one formerly known as 'Jubilee Hotel', which is right opposite the central cinema hall. They make their own bread there. The original owner of the hotel had leased it to *Reza Khan*, who, like us, was also from Mardan. He hired my brother, who then was working there every day, from six o'clock in the morning until nine or ten o'clock in the night. On my brother's request *Reza Khan* employed me as a waiter. As far as I remember there were four or five of us, all from Mardan. I was the youngest and every one looked after me. *Shabash Khan*, the one-eyed night guard, was like a father to me since my brother had barely any time. It was hard work: we had to serve the food, scrub the tables, clean up in the evening and help to wash the heavy cooking pots. Food and lodging was for free. All of us children slept together in a large room just behind the prayer platform. Once a year we went home. This took place during Ramadan, because the hotel remained closed and everything was repainted. Later my younger brother *Irfan* also joined us. I took care of him, because by that time *Kamran* had found a job in 'Kashmir Inn' in Rawalpindi.

I left 'Pathan Hotel' after three years. Someone had shot and robbed *Reza Khan* as he went home in the evening with the day's earnings. He survived, but was badly wounded and so scared that he did not want to work as the manager anymore. With the new manager we had fights all the time. He was a greedy man and a hard task master, constantly hurrying us as if we were chickens. So, I quit and started working in a hotel in Gakuch, which had been opened by a man from Swat. Earlier he'd had a shop in Sazin bazaar, but he could not get along with the Kohistanis there. I was his only help and had to do everything, while he cooked and collected the money. The hotel did not do well, and then he also was opposed to let me go home during Ramadan, insisting that in this way we would miss the best business period of the year. So, I quit again. Actually, I wanted to join my brother in Rawalpindi and find a better job there, but when I arrived, he was so busy with his job that he could not help me with anything.

Then I went back to Gilgit and started working in 'Medina Hotel', to the manager of which I was introduced by a friend from my 'Pathan Hotel' times. Here, I am a waiter now but I am also allowed to help with the cooking in order to learn something more. I never went to school, I can't read and write and I do not know any other trade. Maybe I can become a cook later. Then, when I have earned enough money, I will open my own hotel together with both of my brothers."

Gilgit, April-May 1995

Other trades and professions in which (mostly temporary migrant) Pashto speakers were engaged, included the sale of shoes, the repairing of mechanical, electrical and electronic items, wholesale trade in timber, mobile trade in knives, the running of slaughterhouses for buffaloes and the butcher shops associated with them as well as professional money lending. As for the last business, it was said of a Pathan lender that he would give you any amount of money at any time, but would not hesitate to claim, cut and sell your last tree while collecting his interest on the loan.

When I was enquiring about recent migrants working as farmers I was repeatedly ensured by long-term Pashtun residents that according to their knowledge no one of this occupation had settled in the area since a very long time. This information was somehow corroborated by my own observations, as I was able to identify only two Pathan peasants who had established themselves after Independence. The brothers *Abdullah Khan* and

*Rizwan Khan* originated in Swat, from where they had fled in fear of blood revenge to the Tangir Valley in the 1950s. After placing themselves under the protection of an influential community leader, they were assigned land for building a house in the village of Shatil, where at the time of my visit in spring 1995 they and members of their family were still working as tenants.

But, it was not only that almost no new farmers had settled over the last 40 years. Even peasant households, the founders of which had come to the area much before Independence, were in the process of gradually diversifying their sources of income, slowly but sure moving away form agriculture. One example of this approach was the family of *Alam Khan* from Astor who had sold the larger part of their farmland to the government and invested the money thus earned into setting up a pharmacy in Gilgit bazaar. Another case under consideration was *Sayed Rahman*. As we already know from a previous chapter, his grandfather, *Sayed Emtiyaz,* had acquired fallow land in Chamurga sometime during the end of the colonial period. Later, in the 1960s *Sayed Rahman*'s father had started a business

*Office employee from Sultanabad*

*Karakoram Highway in the upper part of Hunza Valley*

in Gilgit, moving with wife and children to the town and leasing his for Northern Area standards rather considerable piece of arable land to local farmers and members of the Maruts gold washer community. In the time of my research, *Sayed Rahman* and his eldest son, by now owners of two profitable shops in Gilgit's Kashmiri Bazaar, had finally decided to put their Chamurga property for sale, with the aim to invest the money into prospective commercial operations.

What remains to be mentioned regarding professions pursued by Pashtun migrants in the mid 1990s are careers linked to state institutions and the armed services. The unbroken popularity of these kind of positions was as ever connected to the stable income, the high prestige and the right to pension associated with them. But, differently from the past, when, as we saw, such appointments were often given to newly arrived migrants, now only members of well-established, permanent households would be considered as eligible candidates. From among the migrant families mentioned in this study, two grand-sons of the old-time Ghizar merchant *Sarwar Khan* served as officers in the Pakistani army and a third one was working as physician in a local dispensary. One of the brothers of *Abdul Qayyum*, whose father had been working as a mobile trader in Bagrot, held the position of a clerk in the local administration. A brother-in-law of *Nizamuddin* from Skardu was employed in the governmental Forest Department, and a brother of the trader and Chamurga land owner *Sayed Rahman* was a surgeon in Gilgit hospital. Other permanent migrants worked in the Health and Education Departments, in the police service and as teachers in local schools.

# Part 3

# Pashto, Urdu and the others

## 3.1 Using Pashto: Who, when and how

For permanently settled migrants, communication in Pashto was primarily concentrated amongst their own family.[30]

Almost all older interviewees stated that they used Pashto on a regular basis with their parents, wives and children. The only exceptions noted involved cases where the informant's wife was not a native Pashto speaker. In these households, the spouses used to communicate with each other in the wife's mother tongue, usually at the same time the local majority language. However, I was also informed about a few cases where non-Pathan women who had been married into a Pashtun household had picked up Pashto and were using it, parallel to their mother tongue, in communication with their new relatives.

In this context it should be pointed out that in the mid 1990s marriages between Pashtun men and non-Pashtun women were a rather rare phenomenon.[31] On enquiry, I was told that the motive behind such matrimonial unions was the often exorbitant price demanded for a 'real' Pashtun bride. Thus, mixed marriages were almost exclusively limited to the lower-income layer of the permanent Pashto-speaking migrants. In households which had accepted non-Pathan women over two or more generations children tended to grow up with the language of their mother. However, in three such cases recorded by me, the (also) Pashto-speaking fathers had made a conscious effort to impart to their children at least a rudimentary knowledge of their paternal ancestors' tongue.

---

30  This part of the study is based on data pertaining to a selection of 60 interviewees, 30 of them being temporary Pashtun migrants and 30 permanent ones. Both groups were then further subdivided into younger (until 30 years of age) and older speakers.

31  Family histories and socio-linguistic evidence (see also the table in the annex) suggest that this must have been different in the past.

This much about the older generation of permanently settled Pashto speakers. As for the younger migrants, their language situation within the family presented itself in a slightly more differentiated way. Every single informant in this group acknowledged using Pashto while communicating with his father. Children of a non-Pashtun mother generally talked to her in her mother tongue. Siblings normally used Pashto with each other within the home, but while outdoors often chose the local majority language, even if both their parents were Pashto speakers. The common explanation given for this switch was that it took place out of consideration for non-Pashto speakers present during the conversation. However, according to my own observations, the choice was more often than not also motivated by a quantitatively and qualitatively restricted level of mother tongue proficiency among the younger speakers. Actually, on a number of occasions I overheard youngsters at their home talking in Pashto to each other, but changing into the local majority language the moment their elders left the room.

Beyond the inner family circle, it was the neighbours who prevailed for both younger and older permanent migrants as Pashto communication partners. This was especially true in places like Chilas Town and Taus where a number of Pathan households were situated close to each other. While older speakers did not leave any doubt that they preferred to use their common mother tongue with all their Pashtun neighbours, younger informants saw nothing unusual in talking to their friends in the local majority language. However, their friends' fathers and uncles were normally addressed in Pashto.

Regarding temporary Pashtun migrants, who were normally encountered in the local bazaars, the majority of permanently settled speakers stated that they always communicated with them in Pashto. Even the representatives of the younger generation, whose Pashto proficiency was rather low and who would probably have had much less difficulty expressing themselves in Urdu, considered the idea of talking to their non-settled counterparts in any language other than their common mother tongue as 'shameful'.

Temporary Pashtun migrants stated that their most frequent Pashto communication partners came from among fellow residents in their temporary *dēra* households, people who as a rule originated from the same dialectal area as them. Further contacts concerned other temporary migrants encountered while performing professional activities in the bazaar. Dealings with permanently settled Pashto speakers – mostly in their function as customers – were of a much less common nature. Although the communication with them did not seem to pose any major linguistic challenges, a number of temporary migrants complained about the settlers' 'faulty Pashto', especially with regard to the language spoken by the younger generation.

As far as written communication is concerned, only a minority among the Pashtuns included in this study had a formal education, and even in these cases schooling rarely went beyond matriculation grade. At the same time, the number of people who had been to school was much higher among permanent than among temporary migrants. This inequality may be connected to the fact that the majority of the former belonged to the higher-income layer of society whereas the bulk of the latter came from lower-income family backgrounds.

Interestingly, the written language acquired in the course of formal education was normally not Pashto, but Urdu, and, if the informant had been attending a religious school – as some of the temporary migrants had done – also a rudimentary Classical Arabic. For the permanent migrants this lack of mother tongue literary skill can be explained by the circumstance that in the Northern Areas there was no possibility at school level to learn how to read and write Pashto. Thus only three out of 15 younger permanent Pashtun migrants were literate in this language, while 14 of them had actually been to school. The three exceptions came from well-off families and had acquired their Pashto reading and writing proficiency from their fathers. All the other formally educated settlers used Urdu for their personal correspondence.

A rather different picture emerges with regard to the temporary migrants. Although, as already mentioned, there were significantly fewer formally educated people among them (13 out of 30), still, more than the half (i.e. seven) of these literate informants could read and write Pashto.[32]

### 3.1.1 Facing the dialectal divide

Pashto has a great number of dialects, which can be united into three or four larger groups.[33] This dialectal grouping is primarily based on criteria linked to systematic sound changes. Besides, there are also significant morphological and lexical differences between the varieties. Even phonologically close dialects within the same group frequently differ from each other in regard to the use of lexemes and idioms. Thus, for an outsider acquainted only with one dialect it is often difficult to understand speakers of others. An extreme, but characteristic example of this is the variety prevalent in South Waziristan, which an uninitiated non-Pashtun listener could easily take for a separate language only vaguely reminiscent of Pashto.

As a matter of fact, these linguistic difficulties are not only faced by outsiders. Even for native speakers of different Pashto dialects it can be a challenge to converse with each other in their common mother tongue, especially since they cannot fall back on a widely diffused normative language, functioning like, for example, Modern Standard English in the contemporary English-speaking context. However, in the course of their daily interactions Pashtuns have developed certain verbal communication techniques which enable them to cross the existing dialectal boundaries and to communicate successfully in Pashto.

Later on in the text I shall deal with the peculiarities of these commu-

---

32 Taking into consideration the fact that all thirteen had attended a school in the Pashtun core areas, the question naturally arises why only seven of them had mastered their mother tongue – a language with a well established literary tradition – in written form. The main reason for this was obviously that the political decision makers in Pakistan's Pashtun regions did not give much attention to the promotion of Pashto at school level. Along with underpaid, overworked teachers, parents with other educational priorities and the lack of a national literary standard this resulted in a situation where Pashto as a written language was confined to an existence in the shadows.

33 On dialectal divisions of Pashto see Henderson; as well as Skjærvø, pp. 386-387; and Hallberg, 1992a, pp. 16-19.

*Porter from Swabi in Gilgit Bazaar*

nication techniques, as they manifested themselves in the verbal interactions of the Pashtun migrants in the Northern Areas. But first, some observations on the speakers' dialectal origins and their related linguistic choices within their own household.

As will be remembered from the preceding chapters all interviewed Pashto-speaking migrants, permanent and temporary alike, could trace their family roots back to the Pashtun heartland. Most of my informants or their forefathers originally hailed from the predominantly Pashto-speaking region south of Chitral, demarcated in the west by the Pakistani-Afghan border (Durand line), in the south by the Kabul River and in the east by the Indus. From within this region many temporary migrants as well as the majority of migrants settled in the Northern Areas belonged to the valleys of Dir and Swat, to Bajaur and the Mohmand Agency. A significant number of temporary migrants were also from the Malakand Agency as well as from the Swabi and Mardan Districts. Others came from Peshawar District or from the Hazara Subdivision of NWFP, situated on the eastern bank of the Indus. In all these places, the northeastern dialect continuum of Pashto is spoken. A comparatively smaller number of temporary migrants came from regions covered by southeastern dialectal varieties, like from the Bannu and Kohat Districts, from the Kurram Agency, from Waziristan and Baluchistan. A few settled families named eastern Afghanistan as the native place of their ancestors.

Within the migrants' households visited by me, people normally spoke only one dialect, usually identified by them as 'our Pashto'. In the case of temporary migrants this seemed to be the natural choice, since, as already mentioned, a *dēra* was normally shared by people belonging to the same dialect area, if not even to the same family.[34]

Also permanent migrants preferred the company of their kinsmen, taking, whenever possible, marriage partners from within their own clan or tribe. So, it wasn't surprising that most of them had retained the Pashto dialect imported by their forefathers. What was remarkable though, was the rather old-fashioned form they had preserved. Older Pashto speakers, especially, were perfectly aware of this phenomenon. Some of them mentioned with no little pride that only they and their family still used the 'correct' version of their dialect, while the Pashto now spoken in the native region of their ancestors had over the years become 'impure', as witnessed by the mixed-up language of the temporary migrants originating from there.

Whenever Pashto was put into writing, the informant, no matter if permanent or temporary migrant, simply transferred his particular dialect to paper.

Outside their households all Pathan migrants involved in this study regularly came into contact with speakers of other Pashto varieties. Taking into account the in part rather considerable differences between the dialects, one would expect the verbal interaction of their speakers to be seriously hampered by incomprehension and misunderstandings. But this did

---

34   A detailed analysis of the family relationships within a typical Pathan *dēra* household in Gilgit in the mid 1990s can be found in Sökefeld 1998b, p. 286f.

not seem to be the case. As far as I could observe, communication between Pashto migrants using (even very) dissimilar varieties of their mother tongue went on in a smooth and undisturbed way. This apparent ease was achieved by the speakers through following a simple pattern: Each participant in conversation used his own dialect. If the person addressed indicated that he had not understood something which the other had said, the person speaking provided a synonym or a phrase which was intended to illustrate the meaning of his words. In fact, very often the speaker added his explanation not just on request, but immediately after a word or statement, identified by him as potentially creating difficulties in comprehension. The relevant synonym could be taken from the speaker's native dialect or from any other variety, preferably the one spoken by the conversation partner; the explanatory phrase was normally given in the speaker's dialect.

In order to illustrate this approach, below is a short sample recorded during a casual conversation between a shopkeeper from Mardan and his newly engaged assistant from Dir:

*Za, bāzār-na mā-ta pəy rāwra. pəy. tāso če war-ta šodə wāyəy. sə če čāy-kxe āčəy.*

"Go, bring me *pəy* (milk) from the bazaar. *pəy* (milk). What you call *šodə* (milk). What one adds to tea."

This synonym technique, which was also applied by Pashto speakers beyond the Northern Areas, might seem awkward at first but in practice it worked well, without any discernible slowing down of the interaction. Moreover, it was always something special to see how quickly speakers of various Pashto dialects were able to adapt to each other and how fast most of them could activate a whole series of appropriate dialectal synonyms for any given term as and when the need for it arose. Actually, none of the Pashtuns interviewed by me stated that he could not communicate in his native dialect with other Pashto speakers.

It was interesting to observe that even Pashtuns who regularly interacted with speakers of another particular dialect and had therefore acquired

*Cloth merchants from Skardu's New Bazaar*

a good passive knowledge of it, still preferred to use their native variety in conversations with them. When asked about the reason for their choice, they stated that it was better to speak one's own Pashto well and, if necessary, to explain certain things than to make oneself look ridiculous with an incorrect application of the Pashto used by others.

An exception to the synonym technique was made if the conversation partners were able and willing to switch to the so-called Peshawar dialect. This Pashto variety, which is based on the Yusufzai dialect of the people in Swat, enjoyed a high prestige among the speakers of the northeastern continuum.[35] Besides this, it was the standard medium of Peshawar radio, television and newspapers. Among the Pashtuns in the Northern Areas the Peshawar dialect was employed as a kind of supra-regional language. Especially speakers of radically different dialects preferred it while interacting with each other, while conversation partners with northeastern dialectal background often combined its use with the synonym technique.

---

35 The description of a forerunner of the contemporary Peshawar dialect is given in D.L.R. Lorimer's "Syntax of Colloquial Pashto".

Another way to facilitate cross-dialectal communication could have been to fall back on Urdu, Pakistan's *lingua franca*, which, as we shall see further down, was also fairly widespread among Northern Areas' Pashto migrants. However, the recourse to Urdu in such situations was very rare, and limited to the occasional inclusion of an additional word into the speaker's listing of synonyms. The interviewees had their own explanation for this restraint, reasoning that if a compatriot was so uneducated not to understand synonyms even in his own language, there was only little chance that the meaning of the Urdu equivalent could be known to him.

So, how does it come, that the synonym technique and the supra-regional variety were such common and efficient means for cross-dialectal communication between the Pashtun migrants in the Northern Areas? As far as my observations go, the main reasons for this were the following: First of all, conversations outside the speaker's native dialect (i.e. outside the sphere of his own household), at least the conversations witnessed by me, were as a rule limited to simple, everyday situations. Besides this, because of their mobile professional lifestyle many temporary migrants had acquired a high degree of linguistic flexibility in dealing with speakers of Pashto dialects different from their own. And, last but not least, it should be kept in mind that most Pashtuns living in the Northern Areas were native speakers of dialects belonging to the northeastern continuum, a fact which naturally furthered the use of the supra-regional variety.[36]

And still, not withstanding all these favourable conditions, even a casual conversation between speakers of closely related dialects could have its pitfalls. An illustration of the kind of difficulties to be encountered is given in the following account of *Dilraj*, an employee in a Gilgit hotel, whose life story we are already acquainted with from a previous chapter:

> "In my early years in Gilgit, my brother and I used to work in 'Pathan Hotel'. Most of the people employed there were, like us, from Mardan. So we had no difficulties talking to each other. But

---

36 The existence of a *third* cross-dialectal communication tool, a colloquial language/sociolect *specific* to the Northern Areas' Pashto-speaking migrants, as referred to by E. Bauer (1998, pp. 635-639), could not be confirmed from my own material.

I used to have problems understanding the guests' Pashto. Especially the one spoken in Quetta is completely different from ours; but even people from Swat use quite strange expressions. One of them once told me that he had brought some *kaǰūre* for me but then gave me what we in Mardan normally call *γunzāxī* (deep fried biscuits). I had thought he would have brought dates, as this is what *kaǰūre* means for us in Mardan, and was rather disappointed with these oily biscuits. Another guest asked me, while eating, to bring him some *kaŝmīrī*. I was puzzled and went to my brother to ask him what sort of Kashmiris this might be. He explained to me that some people from Swat used this expression for tomatoes. We in Mardan simply say *ṭəmaṭər*.

Also another confusing situation I remember quite well. A boy called *Mohammad Salim* from Mingaora in Swat used to work with us in that time. One day after dinner the two of us were sitting together in our room and talking. Suddenly the door opened and a guest came in. It was an elderly Hajji with a long beard and a shaved upper lip, probably a trader passing through Gilgit. He was looking for my brother, who was supposed to arrange something for him in his room. My brother was still busy at the bakery and I offered to take the Hajji there. Before we left the room he turned towards my friend and asked him: *alaka tə dəlta-kxe sə kawe* ('And what are you doing here, boy?') *Salim* answered: *wali na*. The man said: *xa xa xa ṭīk šu*. ('Good, good, good, that's fine'). At that moment I was perplexed by this short exchange. For me *Salim's* answer *wali na* ('Why shouldn't I be here?') was impolite and irreverent. That was not how I knew *Salim*. And, what was even more bewildering, was the fact the guest accepted *Salim's* impudent words without any remark. The next day I told my brother about the incident and he laughed a lot. Actually, people in Swat use *wali na* when we in Mardan would say *assi* ('Nothing in particular; just so'). That's why *Salim's* answer had seemed rude and disrespectful only to me, while it was perfectly normal for the guest, who also originated from Swat. Later, I heard similar exchanges on many occasions and got accustomed to them. But even then, were somebody from Swat to ask me today what I am doing here, I would always answer with *assi. wali na* is simply too harsh for my ears".

Gilgit, October 1996

All in all, the different approaches towards cross-dialectal communication chosen by Pashtun migrants in the Northern Areas during the time of my research are probably best summarized with the following statement of *Maqbali Khan*, a trader from Mardan, temporarily residing in Gilgit:

"Basically, all of us Pashtuns speak the same language. We only have to get used to the words of the others."

## 3.1.2 Language maintenance: Means and opportunities

There were only limited possibilities for permanently settled Pashto speakers to come into contact with their mother tongue outside their family sphere. The medium of instruction in local schools was usually Urdu, or, in the first grades, the respective majority language. Pashto newspapers, books or other publications were not available in the bazaar. Radio and television programmes transmitted from the traditional Pashtun core areas could not be received.

Only one informant claimed to regularly listen to Pashto language radio news aired by foreign short wave stations. Besides this, there was an hour-long Pashto entertainment programme broadcast once a week on the Pakistani National Television channel (for the few households which had a TV set), the occasional (and usually abysmally bad) Pashto feature film in the cinema halls of Gilgit and Skardu, and, of course interactions with other speakers. But, while it was true that many permanent Pashto-speaking migrants had contacts with their temporary counterparts, these interactions were much more frequent for people in urban areas than in the country side.

As already mentioned, many of the 30 permanent migrants included in this study had been to school, but only three of them were able to read and write in their mother tongue. All the others used Urdu for this purpose. Although in Pakistan Urdu and Pashto share an almost identical script, there was little inclination even among the linguistically and culturally more sensitive settled informants to familiarize themselves with the alphabet of their mother tongue and, based on that, to read Pashto publications. Hardly any of the interviewees knew Pashto poems or folklore. When asked about fairytales, those cited all belonged to local tradition and rendering them in Pashto normally proved difficult, because it was in the respective majority language that one was familiar with them.

All this was completely different in the case of temporary migrants. Because of their strong ties to the bazaar most of them found themselves even outside their shared residences most of the time in Pashto-speaking surroundings. Besides this, almost all of them used to see their families in the traditional Pashtun core areas at least once a year for several weeks. About half of the respondents had been to a school or madrasa in their native villages and a number of them could read and write Pashto. Even if only a small minority of them were interested in mother tongue publications, there were many temporary migrants who, irrespective of their level of formal education, showed acquaintance with Pashto poetry and folklore. Upon inquiry, one usually got to hear popular sayings and poems by Rahman Baba. Typically Pashtun fairytales and anecdotes were also widely known and appreciated.

## 3.2   Urdu as a communication tool

All Pashto speakers interviewed stated that apart from their mother tongue they knew one or more other languages. The most frequently named among them was Urdu.

Although only about 8% of Pakistan's population count it as their mother tongue, Urdu is the country's official language. In this role it is used in all state institutions as well as in schools where it serves as the main medium of instruction. Besides this, by virtue of being a close cognate of Hindi, it offers a vital clue to popular Indian culture which is, mainly in the form of Bollywood movies and songs, accessed and appreciated by all strata and communities of Pakistani society. And, most important for our study, because of its high prestige and wide circulation, Urdu also functions as Pakistan's main communication language, its *lingua franca*.

All formally educated Pashto speakers interviewed stated that they could read and write Urdu. As a medium for private correspondence it was used by more than half of the temporary and by all but three of the permanent literate migrants.

A vast majority of informants claimed that they knew enough Urdu to handle all aspects of their professional life. At the same time, a speaker's actual language proficiency varied strongly depending on his level of formal education, his occupational milieu and his degree of mobility. Thus, longer schooling periods, extensive contacts with non-Pashto speaking communication partners and an elevated degree of professional mobility usually led to a better knowledge of Urdu.

However, having said this, it must also be acknowledged that the general level of Urdu proficiency among the encountered Pashtun migrants did not seem excessively high. In fact, all over the Northern Areas Pashtuns were rather famous for speaking Urdu in a rough and clumsy way. This impression mainly arose from their persistent habit to de-aspirate aspirates and to de-nasalize nasals as well as from their inclination towards confusing the grammatical gender of certain verb forms; all this, no doubt, under the influence of their East Iranian mother tongue.

Most of my informants were well aware of their Urdu shortcomings, without, however, considering actually improving them. The majority simply did not bother with correct Urdu pronunciation or a proper application of grammatical rules. Instead, they appeared absolutely satisfied with simply making themselves understood.

At the same time, the interviewees did not seem to exhibit any special inertia or unwillingness towards learning Urdu as such. It was just "all about the right amount", as one of them aptly put it. Here is an example of how this attitude was reflected in daily practice: Predictably, the least acquainted with Urdu were younger temporary migrants with no formal education, who had left their home village in search of work for the very first time. On several occasions I could observe how during the early

*Shina-speaking herdsmen from Tangir Valley*

weeks of their stay in the area such newcomers made great efforts to absorb from their surroundings enough Urdu to be able to have a professional exchange with their non-Pathan customers. However, as soon as they had reached their self-designated level of Urdu competence, they typically lost interest in learning the language any further. The result of this strongly utilitarian rapport with Urdu was a very simplified 'bazaar version' of the language, which in its characteristic Pashtun-style interpretation could be clearly set apart from colloquial varieties spoken by members of other ethno-linguistic groups.[37]

---

37   Another interesting feature of my informants' Urdu use was that all of them, even the ones whose proficiency in this language was otherwise only very superficial, were perfectly capable of counting in it. This ability was especially noticeable in interactions involving calculations with money, where Pashtuns used Urdu numbers not only with non-Pashtuns but also while dealing with each other. The habit – to be observed also in the Pashtun core areas – is the more remarkable since in Pashto compound numbers are far easier to construct than in Urdu, where their morphological structure is not transparent anymore and one is thus compelled to learn the first hundred units by heart.

As could be expected, many informants named the bazaar as the place where they had learnt to speak Urdu. The bazaar was also the location where temporary migrants cultivated the language as their most important medium of communication with non-Pashto speakers. For permanent migrants, though, Urdu here ranked only second after the local majority language.[38]

## 3.3  Local languages: Attitudes, use and influence on Pashto

Differently from Urdu, in respect of which permanent and temporary migrant Pashto speakers shared more or less the same attitudes, their opinions diverged significantly when it came to their relationship with locally spoken languages.

Only a very small number of the interviewed temporary migrants revealed familiarity with any of the local languages current in the Northern Areas. Many informants did not even know the common name of the majority language spoken in their immediate neighbourhood. If asked about it, they usually came up with geographically determined, descriptive terms like *gilgitī* "Gilgitian", *də punyal jibə* "the language of Punyal" or *də astoriyāno jibə* "the language of the people from Astor".

Consequently, these migrants depended entirely upon Urdu for their dealings with speakers of local languages. But, interestingly, hardly anybody interviewed seemed to consider his thus rather limited ability to communicate as a serious handicap. First of all, as claimed by the informants, local customers usually knew enough Urdu to allow both sides an oral exchange in business matters. And second, as I observed myself on various occasions, temporary migrants' private interactions with non-Pashtuns were normally limited to the simplest routine situations. In this context it is not surprising that none of the temporary migrants interviewed stated that they had regular personal contacts with members of

---

38   Urdu, besides English was usually also mentioned as the most preferred language that my informants would like their children to master besides their mother tongue. The generally given explanation for this choice was that proficiency in English and/or Urdu opened the door to well paid, prestigious jobs and would thus provide their children with a chance for a better life.

autochthonous groups and only few admitted the thought that familiarity with one of the Northern Areas' vernaculars could be of any use to them.

As a matter of fact, an overwhelming majority of temporary Pashtun migrants exhibited a strongly critical opinion of the local inhabitant's culture and way of life. This not always unbiased attitude was normally also extended to the peoples' languages, which, on account of their being phonetically very different from Pashto and Urdu must have appeared rather alien to the Pashtun ear. The following words of *Wajahat Bangash*, trader of electric goods in Gilgit bazaar, can be taken as a typical expression of the temporary migrants' state of mind:

> "By selling our goods to these wretched mountain dwellers, we are giving them the opportunity to link themselves to the big world outside. They need us. Why should we care about them, why should we learn their language?"

The only temporary migrants who demonstrated a certain amount of interest in the local idioms were traders and craftsmen operating as mobile entrepreneurs outside fixed bazaar structures. In the course of their journeys from village to village they used to come into contact with women and old people, who, because of their low degree of mobility and limited access to formal education, often had no knowledge of Urdu. During such encounters familiarity with a local language could be crucial for the trader's commercial success. Thus travelling entrepreneurs, who had been for some years engaged in trade and crafts in remote valleys, were the only temporary Pathan migrants acquainted with at least some words and functional expressions in a local language.

In sharp contrast to the temporary migrants, permanently settled Pashtuns were usually well familiar with the vernaculars spoken around them. For all of them the majority language of their place of living was the most important medium of communication with members of other ethno-linguistic groups. Urdu, so much relied upon by the temporary migrants, came only second or third. All migrants born in the Karakoram spoke at least one of the local languages, regardless of whether they lived in urban centres or in rural areas. In some families, like the one of *Yasin*

*Khan*, a 26-year-old Gilgit resident, besides Pashto and Urdu three, four or even more local idioms were mastered:

> "The family of my father, whom everybody here knows as *Yunus Kabari*, is originally from Bajaur. My grandfather *Mohammad* came to this region about 80 years ago. Initially he and his eldest son were engaged in mobile trade in Gupis and Yasin. Later he opened a shop in Gupis and settled down. Also my father was born there. In my grandfather's house everybody spoke Pashto. My grandfather also knew some Khowar since he had worked in Chitral earlier. As a child my father like all his brothers learned to speak Shina and Khowar while playing with local friends. This knowledge proved to be very useful for him when he was travelling as a trader through the valleys or working in my grandfather's shop.
>
> My mother's father is the second son of *Fazil Rahman Khan*, who fled with his family from Yarkand in China in the 1950s and came here to Pakistan. I remember clearly that all the family members in my maternal grandfather's house spoke beside Pashto also Uighur. My mother knows this language very well. But now that both her parents have passed away she only uses it to converse with her sisters in situations when they don't want to be understood by the rest of us. Sometime after Partition one of my father's younger brothers, uncle *Mahbub*, had acquired land in Taus Village in the Yasin Valley. He built a house, opened a shop and settled there. One of his sons today speaks the local [Werchikwar-] Burushaski. He learnt it in the course of his business trips to upper Yasin. Burushaski is a very difficult language and only a few Pashtuns here have a command over it. Actually, I am the only Pashtun in Gilgit to know Burushaski. I picked it up from my playmates as a child.
>
> Apart from that, I and my brother naturally know Shina, and then also Urdu and English. Shina is the language of Gilgit and everybody in our household speaks it fluently. All men in the family

know Urdu, and my sister too, since she has received an education. But only my brother and I learnt English in school. If we count now: Pashto, Shina, Burushaski, Khowar, Uighur, Urdu and English – seven tongues are spoken in our family. Sometimes I wonder which will be the language of my children."

Gilgit, July 1996

In keeping with their geographical and numerical distribution through the Northern Areas, the most widespread local language current among permanent Pashtun migrants, as exemplified here by the family of *Yasin Khan*, was Shina. Pathans settled in Ghizar District often (besides Shina also) spoke Khowar. Balti was the second language of Pashto speakers settled in Skardu. In comparison, proficiency in Burushaski was rather low: some informants from Taus spoke its Werchikwar dialect and the quoted *Yasin Khan* could communicate in its Hunza variety. Interestingly, none of the interviewees showed any knowledge of Wakhi, probably because there were no permanent migrants' households in the areas where it was used as a majority language.

Since the relevant local language was normally acquired in early childhood, Pashtuns born in the Northern Areas were usually as proficient in it as the native speakers. Such widespread bilingualism often fostered situations, especially involving young people, in which the actual mother tongue took a back-seat as the medium of communication. As already mentioned, it was not unusual to see siblings, both parents of whom were Pashtuns, communicating with each other in the local majority language, and using their native tongue only while talking with or in the presence of older family members. When asked to explain their choice the speakers sometimes stated that they preferred the local language since they could express themselves "faster" and "more clearly" in it.

It will come as no surprise that this kind of complete bilingualism exercised a strong influence on the Pashto spoken by younger permanent migrants. First of all, one could note a tendency towards simplification and standardisation, which found its expression among other things in the adaptation of irregular morphological forms to what could be per-

*Farmer's son from Bassin (Gilgit District)*

ceived to be the 'correct' Pashto norm (e.g. *šina čāy* instead of *šna čāy* "green tea"; *rorān* instead of *rūṇa* "brothers") as well as in the avoidance of subordinate clauses. Besides this, interference from local languages (in the observed cases always from Shina) resulted in the frequent replacement of original Pashto lexemes with ad-hoc loans; in the establishment of congruence between agent and predicate in the ergative construction (untypical for Pashto, where in this case the verb is coordinated with the direct object); and in the application of this construction to statements in the present tense.

However, these modifications only concerned the speakers' individual language. According to my observations, there were no systematic differences, which would have allowed to define the form of speech current among permanent migrants in the Northern Areas as a separate (sub-) variety of Pashto.

## 3.4 Pashto as mother tongue: A pragmatic choice

While it was out of question that temporary migrants might eventually give up their mother tongue Pashto for any of the local languages, regarding their permanent counterparts the situation appeared anything but clear.

On the one hand there were some clear signs indicating that in the course of time a number of households could further reduce the use of Pashto and finally exchange it for the respective majority language. Among these signs one may count the rather restricted use of Pashto beyond the family sphere and the wide-spread phenomenon of bilingualism, encountered on all levels of the speakers' community. Actually, for a number of individuals the process of language change was already rather advanced. One might only think about those youngsters who used to switch whenever possible to the local majority language, or elderly Pathans, who spoke Pashto only rarely, maybe once per week, while talking to a trader, or a relative in a nearby village.

On the other hand, the above tendencies were somehow belied by a remarkable continuity in the use of Pashto within the family. So, our table (see annex) indicates that out of 18 households with children only three did not pass on their mother tongue to the next generation. Moreover, even if we look at families founded on mixed marriages, only in two out of five the children grew up exclusively with their mother's language. And last but not least, when directly asked about how they perceived the prospects of their mother tongue in the Northern Areas, many interviewees would answer in the spirit of the following statement made by *Dilawar Khan*, a shop owner from Gupis:

> "Pashto was the language of our grandfathers. Pashto is the language of our fathers. How can our children call themselves Pashtuns if they do not master their language? How can they preserve their pride without Pashto?"

Taking all this into consideration one would probably not be wrong in assuming that over the coming decades a number of households will lose Pashto, while others will retain it. So far, so good. But which factors would be decisive for loss or retention? And would the result be determined by a more or less conscious decision or rather be dictated by circumstances out of an individual's control?

To attempt an answer to these questions we should shortly return to the Pashtun migrants' settlement history. As it will be remembered in connection with the recollections of *Muhammad Isa* from Tarishing, the Northern Areas' villages were home to a number of families or family groups, who were still referred to as 'Pathan' by their neighbours, but had (almost) given up Pashto in favour of a local language. Comparing these permanent households with those which were still fully Pashto-speaking, it appeared that the basic feature which distinguished them from each other was their economic situation.

All the households effected by mother tongue change were situated in rural settings. They were making their living predominantly from agriculture and (thus) had a relatively low income. In the Northern Areas, like in many other places affected by modernisation, the economic standing of a household was a major and often decisive factor in determining its social status. As far as their financial means were concerned, these low-income families did not differ much from their local neighbours, who like them were farmers living hand to mouth. The only characteristic which in the eyes of their co-villagers set them apart from the rest of the settlement and accorded them a comparatively lower social position was their 'foreignness' – the fact that they as 'Pathans' did not belong to the traditional population of the region. The most explicit, and in many cases the only remaining outward sign of this 'foreignness' was their distinctive language. Consequently, the concerned settlers tended to perceive their original mother tongue Pashto as nothing but a hurdle, the last barrier that had to be removed on their way to full integration, a tolerable price to pay for a better social standing.

A totally different situation presented itself in the case of these permanently settled migrant families, who, although also fully bilingual, still employed Pashto on an equal footing with the local majority language and did not show any tendency towards mother tongue change. The bread winners of almost all these households were traders or employees. They lived primarily in the economic centres of the region, had a good, often above average, income and, linked to that, normally wielded a fair amount of social influence. Their distinctive standing in the local community was further underpinned by the physical and financial presence of their temporary migrating compatriots, the position of the neighbouring Pashto speaking NWFP as an economic and (primarily for Indus Diamer) cultural reference point, as well as by the popular Pakistani perception of Pathans as hard-working, but also brutal, stubborn and self-centred tribal warriors. This combination of money, social influence and image made the Pashto speakers settled in the Northern Areas a social group seldom loved but generally held in respect and treated with a certain distance. Membership of this group was established through the identification of the concerned person as 'Pathan'; which in turn was, according to all interviewees, Pashtuns and non-Pashtuns alike, mainly based on his or her ability to speak Pashto. Consequently, for the settled migrants concerned, the preservation of their mother tongue was hardly just a matter of ethnic sentiments, but had turned into nothing less than a prerequisite for the maintenance of their status in society.

Thus, in the cases observed by me, loss or preservation of Pashto did not primarily depend on opportunities for language maintenance, marriage patterns of the speakers, the geographic distribution of their households, or some abstract notion of identity. Of course, all these factors will have played their role, but the key to the issue was the speakers' attitude towards the 'usefulness' of their mother tongue in determining their social position within their host community.

For one, comparatively smaller group, Pashto had turned into a liability, since it could easily be brought into play by people they had to rely on on a daily basis as an argument for their status as 'outsiders' whose place was to be found on the fringes of the local community, on the lower half of the social ladder.

For others the preservation of their mother tongue became simply indispensable, since it served as an efficient tool to mark their place within a comparatively affluent, influential and respected population group.

# Part 4

# To be Continued?

Whilst the preceding chapters dealt with the history of Pashtun presence in the Northern Areas and the migrants' situation there during the time of my research, this final part of the study will attempt to outline possible developments in the future. For this I will first sum up characteristic features and trends linked to the Northern Areas' Pashtun migration in the mid 1990s, and than look at how likely these trends are to continue or to change over the coming decades.

## 4.1 Form of migration

Pashtun migration to the Northern Areas occurred in two different forms – a temporary form and a permanent one.

This division can be traced back as far as the second half of the 18th century, as already at that time contemporary accounts mentioned the existence of temporary traders and settled farmers. Later, over the colonial and much of the post-Partition period, most new Pashtun arrivals established their own permanent households. The blood revenge refugees decided on it, as settling for good not only gave them the possibility to earn their living, but also increased the resolve of their hosts to protect them in case of need. Early preachers, too, would have perceived it as an advantage since it created strong bonds with the people whose trust and support was essential for the success of their religious mission. For traders and craftsmen, in turn, a permanent household was, first and foremost, a choice dictated by the remoteness of the area, because regular visits to their native places would have taken up much of their business time on the spot and thus created room for more adaptable competitors.

This trend began to reverse with the construction of the Karakoram Highway. The use of the Highway reduced travel time and travel cost to such an extent, that even the poorest and busiest of entrepreneurs could allow himself to visit his family at least once a year. Besides this, by the

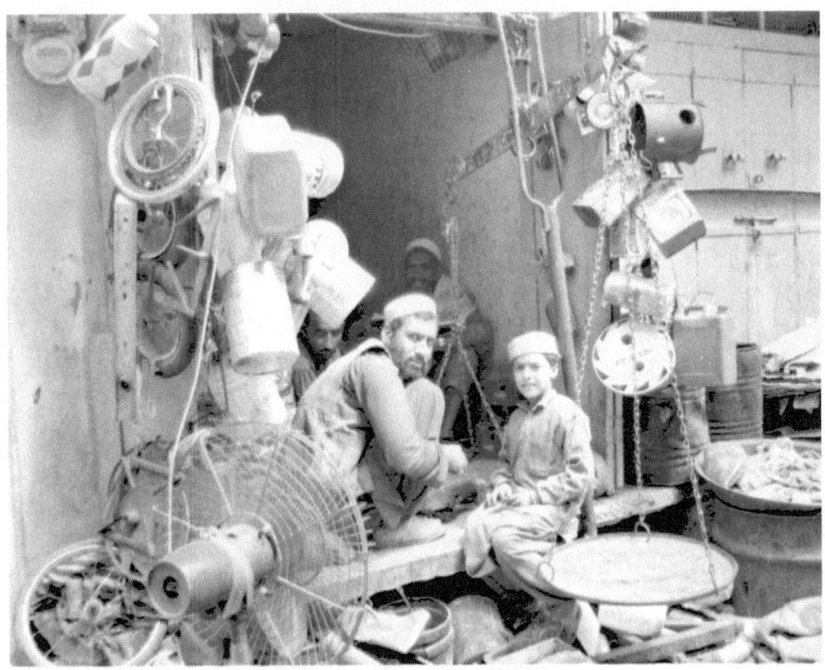
*Dealers with recyclable goods in Skardu*

1970s Pashtun preachers and blood revenge refugees had stopped settling in the area, as the preachers now combined their vocation with trade or a craft; and the blood revenge refugees may have preferred other, less accessible, hideouts.

Due to these factors, in the mid 1990s the absolute majority of migrants, even people who had been working in the Northern Areas already for many years, preferred to stay in a temporary household instead of going through the trouble and the expenses of setting up their own permanent place. Thus, with the reasons for permanent migration having disappeared, its temporary form had become the rule. This is expected to remain the case in the foreseeable future.

## 4.2 Professional activities and geographical distribution

Of all professions carried out by the people living in the Northern Areas, it was trade in which the Pashtun migrants of the mid 1990s were predominantly involved.

This situation had been very similar in the past. Traders were among the first Pashto speakers to reach the area. In the beginning, their activities concentrated on places close to Chitral and Indus Kohistan, neighbouring regions which had already earlier come into the orbit of Pashtun commercial interests.

Until the first decades of the 20th century Pashtun trade activities in the Northern Areas were rather modest. However, over the years, with the steady improvement of the economic environment and the infrastructural set-up, the volume of trade increased. And so did the numbers of Pathan businessmen and their radius of action. Thus, by the mid 1990s stationary Pashto-speaking traders were running shops in all centrally located bazaars, while their mobile counterparts reached out to the more remote villages.

Of course, improved economic conditions also created business opportunities for representatives of other ethno-linguistic groups. During the colonial period Pashtun traders mostly competed with entrepreneurs coming from outside the region (e.g. Kashmir), while the decades after Partition saw a significant increase of locally owned businesses. With the passage of time, growing competition promoted a certain specialisation among traders. In this context most Pashtun entrepreneurs concentrated on a range of items which reflected what had always been their main commercial advantage: the ability to rely on a network of businesses operated by family members or partners beyond the borders of the Northern Areas, including the Pakistani lowlands, Afghanistan and China. Consequently, in the mid 1990s the most successful Pashtun shop owners tended to be those who dealt with products the sale or the purchase of which necessitated direct and regular outside contacts. There is little doubt that this trend will also prevail in the future.

Therefore, over the decades to come, the bazaars in the Northern Areas will almost certainly see a further increase of Pashtun owned shops dealing in all kinds of goods related to the China and Afghanistan trade, as well as with fruits and vegetables from Swat and places further to the south. Besides this, likely to remain are specialised traders in Pakistani light industry products like shoes, fabrics and ready made cloths, as well as the dealers in hides, bones and recyclable material. Less promising are the prospects for non-specialised mobile traders, as they will almost certainly be put out of business by local village shops.

Other professional activities which are most likely to be favoured by Pashto-speaking migrants in the future are certain crafts as well as jobs in the service sector. Among the crafts, the cobbler's work had always been a kind of Pashtun monopoly and will obviously remain so, not least because members of autochthonous ethno-linguistic groups exhibit an almost physical aversion to it. The same is true for the barber's profession, although here Pashto speakers will probably have to continue to compete with other outsiders, presumably, as in the past, Hindko speakers from Hazara.

There is a strong possibility that in line with the economic development of the area the hospitality business will continue to grow. In this context it can be expected that the Pashto speakers' involvement into this sector will increase. Although the future will certainly also see more inns, tea houses and restaurants owned and operated by representatives of other ethno-linguistic groups, there is little doubt that Pashtun migrant workers and travellers will continue to choose Pashtun-run places and Pashtun hotel owners will take care to employ staff who speak the language of their clients.

On the other hand, all indicators point to a further decrease of Pashto-speaking farmer households in the area, as most of those which still existed in the mid 1990s are expected to either assimilate linguistically to their surroundings or to change their main source of income from agriculture to trade.

Closely linked to the Pashtun migrants' professional activities is their distribution across the area. In the past, traders and craftsmen concentrated in central places like Gupis, Gilgit Town and Chilas. Farm households in the countryside still figured prominently in early records, but diminished with time, both in absolute and in proportional terms. Thus, at the beginning of the 1980s there were already six times more Pashto-speaking migrants living in urban centres than in rural areas. Fifteen years later, by the mid 1990s, Pashtun migrants had not only put down roots in Skardu Town, but also established themselves in newly emerging roadside markets along the KKH and the Indus Valley Road. This bazaar-centred distribution pattern of Pashtun migrants is not expected to change in the future.

## 4.3 Language situation and integration

Regarding the migrants' language situation, we will first look at issues connected to their common mother tongue and then discuss their relationship with the local idioms.

In the mid 1990s the Pashto spoken by temporary migrants manifested itself as a living, vigorous language which maintained a close relationship with the dialects of the traditional Pashtun core areas, directly participating in all aspects of their linguistic development.

The Pashto spoken by permanent migrants was on an individual level often 'old fashioned' and/or influenced by local languages. On a systematic level, though, there were no indications that it had transformed into a separate, independent variety.

Also in the future the formation of a Pashto variety *specific* to the Northern Area seems to be very unlikely. First of all, there is no need for it, as the most important function of such a variety in the given context, which would be to facilitate cross-dialectal communication, is already fulfilled by the application of the synonym technique and the use of the Peshawar dialect. Besides this, such a development would be strongly impeded by the open structure of the speakers' community, as permanent and temporary migrants do not exist isolated from each other and the latter are in constant touch with the Pashto varieties spoken in their places of origin.

Similarly improbable is the possibility that Pashto could in the foreseeable future assume the position of a *lingua franca* in (parts of) the Northern Areas. Although exactly this had happened in neighbouring Kohistan and Chitral, the Northern Areas differ from these regions in two important aspects. Firstly, the area does not form part of the Pashto-dominated

NWFP, and secondly, it is not home to ethno-linguistic groups which habitually speak Pashto as a second language.

And last, but not least, some remarks on the migrants' relationship with local languages. In the mid 1990s it was obvious that the different approaches Pashto-speaking migrants took in their relationship with local languages reflected their difference in attitude towards integration into their respective host communities.

One end of the spectrum was represented by those rural low-income households which were in the process of fully embracing the local majority language, turning it into their own mother tongue. Although this process of linguistic, and ultimately also cultural, blending of minority groups into their majority surroundings was characteristic for the area, concerning Pashtuns it was clearly coming to an end, as the prevailing tendency among settled migrants was not to change, but to retain their original mother tongue.

At the other end of the range there were the temporary Pashtun migrants. Most of them did not know anything connected to local languages, and the few who knew at least something, used their limited skills exclusively for business transactions. At the same time, there was a clear tendency, even among people who had been living and working in the area already for many years, to disapprove of basically everything related to the culture and society surrounding them. Their sometimes harsh and arrogant judgements were echoed by the locals, who never hesitated to describe Pathans as greedy, cunning and brutal, as trouble-makers, religious fanatics, professional smugglers and homosexuals, just to name some of the more popular stereotypes. There is no doubt that these kinds of mutual feelings, combined with the possibility of living in a purely Pashto-speaking environment and to work with Urdu, will also in the future give little encouragement to the average temporary Pashtun migrant to learn a local language or even to consider getting any closer to local society.

Between these two extremes were those permanent migrant families who used their mother tongue, Pashto, and the local majority language on an almost equal footing. This consciously maintained bilingualism was

*Residential area in Gilgit*

part of their efforts to position themselves *vis-à-vis* their respective host communities.

Of course, to keep a balance between traditional identity and the new environment was probably never an easy task. But while in the past being a stranger and an insider at the same time had clearly worked to the migrants' advantage, the massive arrival of their compatriots following the opening of the Karakoram Highway had disturbed the delicate equilibrium.

In the mid 1990s local attitudes towards Pashtun migrants were slowly but surely changing from critical to hostile, as they were increasingly perceived as alien elements whose presence was, if not causing, at least worsening existing social problems. Although open expressions of hostility were primarily directed at temporary migrants, few representatives of autochthonous ethno-linguistic groups seemed to be ready to make a clear distinction between them and the Pashto speakers who had been born in the Northern Areas.

My Pashtun conversation partners, especially those settled in Gilgit, a place where religious and economic differences tended to translate into communal violence, were very much aware of these developments. Thus, while discussing the prevailing situation with them I could often discern a certain uneasiness about the prospects of their traditional balancing act. The image they projected to the outside, though, was, as it had always been, one of self-confidence, pride and defiance.

I would like to conclude the present study with a text related to a small incident in Gilgit bazaar, which serves as an illustration of how permanent Pashtun migrants in that town faced the complex social situation prevailing there in the mid 1990s. The story was recorded in December 1996 from the ca. 50-year-old office clerk *Musharraf Khan*:

> "My family is settled in the Northern Areas for more than 70 years. If you look at how we dress and how we live we could be any family here in Gilgit. We speak Shina as fluent as our neighbours, we eat the same food, we celebrate the same holidays, we are happy about the same things and we share the same worries. But in our hearts we are Pashtuns. Our ancestors came from Bajaur, we speak Pashto with our children and everything happening in the places of our forefathers is capturing our interest. In our family we have never made an issue out of this. Pathan, Shin, Yashkun, Sunnite, Ismaili and even Shiite, in the past this did not play any role. What counted was the respect people would give to you, not the language you spoke or the religious sect you belonged to. Of course, there had been problems too, but never this kind of hatred one is encountering nowadays.
> 
> As for me, and probably for most of the other people here, the big change came with the 1988 sectarian clashes. Our family was lucky, nobody was killed or injured, but it was a very scary time. One could easily have been beaten up or even shot dead simply for belonging to the wrong sect. It was in the aftermath of these tragic events that Pathans were accused of inspiring the unrest, or having brought in weapons from down country to make money by selling them to the fighters. I can't speak for all Pashtuns, but

at least I know, that we, who are settled in Gilgit, were as terrified as everybody else, and suffered as much as our neighbours. None of us made profit out of all this, and many of my relatives and friends even lost money as shops remained closed and customers from outside kept away for months.

The 1988 tension was a tragedy for the whole town, but few people have learnt the right lesson from it. If you ask me, since then things have gone from bad to worse. Young people, especially, have become ever more radical in their opinions. And thanks to their foolishness and the hypocrisy of their fathers, once peaceful Gilgit has broken up into hostile neighbourhoods. Shiites speak badly about Sunnites, Sunnites curse Shiites, Ismailis keep away from everybody else, Shins and Yashkuns abuse Kashmiris, Kashmiris harass Dooms and, whenever someone wants to let off steam, Pathans are the favourite target. This kind of behaviour will not work with us, though, at least not openly, as they know we are strong and they are scared of our response, but it's an easy game with the guys who come here to work in the bazaar, who will protect them?

Lately, I went to buy some oranges. When I arrived at my favourite vegetable stall, I witnessed a small incident. Two customers, young men, one of them from our neighbourhood, were accusing the seller, who was a Pathan of their own age, of having tried to cheat them. First, they addressed him directly in Urdu, but very soon they switched to Shina, launching a tirade of abuse against him and Pathans in general. All the time they used very offensive language. Of course, most of the things they said the seller did not understand, but from their intonations and gestures it must have been very clear to him that it was pretty bad. In the beginning, the lad had defended himself, but from the moment they had changed to Shina he just gave them a blank stare. As they did not show any intention of stopping their angry speech or to move away, it was only a matter of time until the seller or one of his friends would respond in kind. And with that there would be a big risk for the situation getting out of control. Because of the noise, people from neighbouring shops were already turning their heads towards us. So, I decided to intervene. I put my hand on the shoulder of the young man next to me and spoke to him, trying to calm him down. He gave me an annoyed look and said: 'But, uncle, it's not about you, it's about them.' And the other added: 'Yes, all these Pathans are just cheaters, all of them, profiting from us, sucking our blood and destroying our peace.' Anyhow, maybe it was because of my grey hair, or maybe because one of them felt embarrassed recognising me as his neighbour, I finally managed to take them away from the shop. After that, I went back to the place and apologised for the young men's behaviour. The shop owner who knew me well, and who had not been present during the incident, smiled and said: 'Please, don't worry for us. We are already used to it. Some people here are really crazy. Lately a man told me: 'You Pathans are shameless, you are doing even the lowest kind of labour just to earn money.' Isn't it strange to blame somebody because he earns his living in a difficult, but honest way?'

By God, it is strange, but what worries me more than these odd accusations is the aggressiveness they are brought forward with. What will I do, if somebody will behave with me or my sons in such a hostile way? Will I be able to swallow my pride and to keep calm like this shopkeeper and his assistant did? Honestly, I prefer not to think about it.

You know, it is obvious that some people here in Gilgit are not happy with our presence. They envy our money and our influence, they despise our habits, they hate our views on religion and who knows what else they are finding fault with. This is an old story, just the form in which it is expressed has changed. According to me, the best we can do, is what we always did, leave them where they are and move on with our own lives, just as the

Pashto proverb goes: 'The dogs are barking and the caravan passes by'. Or, as my late father used to put it: 'They like us, they don't like us, what should we care? We are here now, and we are here to stay.' That's it, nothing else. Full stop."

# Annex

# References

Allan, J. R. N. (1989): Kashgar to Islamabad: the impact of the Karakorum Highway on mountain society and habitat. In: Scottish Geographical Magazine, Vol. 105, No. 3, pp. 1390-141.

Barth, F. (1956): Indus and Swat Kohistan. An Ethnographic Survey. Oslo 1956. (Studies Honouring the Centennial of the Universitetets Etnografiske Museum, Oslo 1857–1957, Vol. II)

Bauer, E. (1998): Several Groups of Pashto-Speakers in Pakistan's Northern Areas: Different Ways of Dealing with Multilingual Surroundings (Preliminary Results of Field Research). In: Stellrecht, I. (ed.): Karakorum-Hindukush-Himalaya, Dynamics of Change, Part II – Culture Area Karakorum, Scientific Studies, Vol 4. II, Köln 1998, pp. 627-640.

Biddulph, J. (1880): Tribes of the Hindoo Koosh. Calcutta 1880 (Reprint: Karachi 1977).

Cacopardo, Alberto (1991) The Other Kalasha. A Survey of Kalashamun-Speaking People in Southern Chitral. Part I: The Eastern Area. In: East and West 41, Rome, pp. 273-310.

Cacopardo, Augusto (1991) The Other Kalasha. A Survey of Kalashamun-Speaking People in Southern Chitral. Part II: The Kalasha of Urtsun. In: East and West 41, Rome, pp. 311-350.

Caroe, Olaf (1958): The Pathans: 550 B.C.–A.D. 1957. Karachi 1958 (numerous reprints)

Dani, A.H. (1989): History of Northern Areas of Pakistan. Islamabad 1989. (Second Edition: Islamabad 1991)

Decker, K. D. (1992): Languages of Chitral. Islamabad 1992 (Sociolinguistic Survey of Northern Pakistan 5).

Decker, S. J. (1992): Ushojo. In: Resch, C. R.; Decker, J. D.; Hallberg, D.G. (eds.): Languages of Kohistan – Sociolinguistic Survey of Northern Pakistan 1, Islamabad 1992, pp. 65-82.

Dittmann, A. (1995): The Bazaars of Gilgit: Ethnic and Economic Determinants of Centrality. In: Stellrecht, I. (ed.): Problems of Comparative High Mountain Research with Regard to the Karakorum – Occasional Papers, No. 2, Tübingen 1995, pp. 118-130.

Dittmann, A. (1997a): Ethnic Groups and Bazaar Economy in Baltistan. In: Dodin, T.; H. Räther (eds.): Recent Research on Ladakh 7 – Ulmer Kulturanthropologische Schriften, Vol. 9, Ulm 1997, pp. 117-134.

Dittmann, A. (1997b): Central Goods and Ethno-Linguistic Groups in the Bazaars of Northern Pakistan: An Example of Central Place Theory Modifications in Mountainous Environments. In: Stellrecht, I.; Winiger, M. (eds.): Perspectives on History and Change in the Karakorum, Hindukush and Himalaya. – Culture Area Karakorum, Scientific Studies, Vol. 3, Köln 1997, pp. 119-133.

Dittmann, A. (1998): Raum und Ethnizität. Konfliktfelder und Koalitionen in multi-ethnischen Bazaren Nordpakistans. In: Grugel, A.; Schröder, I. W. (eds.): Grenzziehungen – Zur Konstruktion ethnischer Identitäten in der Arena sozio-politischer Konflikte – Mosaik der Kulturen, Bd. 2, Frankfurt a.M., pp. 45-78.

Faggi, P.; Ginestri, M. (1977): La rete dei bazar nell'alta valle del l'Indo. In: Rivista Geografica Italiana, Annata LXXXIV, Fasc. 3-4, Firenze, Settembre-Dicembre 1977, pp. 315-349; 428-450.

General Staff India (1928): Military Report and Gazetteer of the Gilgit Agency and the Indpendent Territories of Tangir and Darel. Simla 1928.

Government of Azad Kashmir (1952): Census of Azad Kashmir, 1951. Azad Kashmir, Gilgit & Baltistan, Report & Tables. Murree: 1952.

Hallberg, D.G. (1992a): Pashto, Waneci, Ormuri. Islamabad 1992 (Sociolinguistic Survey of Northern Pakistan 4)

Hallberg, D.G. (1992b): The Languages of Indus Kohistan. In: Resch, C. R.; Decker, J. D.; Hallberg, D.G. (eds.): Languages of Kohistan – Socio-linguistic Survey of Northern Pakistan 1, Islamabad 1992, pp. 83-144

Henderson, M. (1983): Four Varieties in Pashto. In: Journal of the American Oriental Society, Vol. 103, No. 3, pp. 595-597.

Holdschlag, A. (2006): "...*a curious and intricate ethnological puzzle*": Diversität und rezente interkulturelle Interaktionsprozesse im Hochgebirge Nordwestpakistans. Universität Heidelberg. Südasien-Institut. Available at: *www.ub.uni-heidelberg.de/archiv/6369* (Last update 5.6.2007)

Holzwarth, W. (1999): Materialien zur Geschichte des Karakorum und östlichen Hindukusch, 1500–1800. Manuscript. Berlin 1999.

Israr-ud-Din (1969): The people of Chitral: a survey of their ethnic diversity. In: Pakistan Geographical Review, Vol. 24, pp. 45-57.

Jettmar, K. (1960) Soziale und wirtschaftliche Dynamik bei asiatischen Gebirgsbauern (Nordwestpakistan). In: Soziologus, N.F., Jg. 10,2, pp. 120-138.

Jettmar, K. (1961): Ethnological Research in Dardistan 1958. Preliminary Report. In: Proceedings of the American Philosophical Society. Vol. 105, pp. 79-97

Knight, E.F. (1893): Where three Empires Meet. London, 1893 [Reprint: Asian Educational Services 1993]

Kreutzmann, H. (1989): Hunza – Ländliche Entwicklung im Karakorum. Berlin. (Abhandlungen Anthropogeographie. Institut für Geographische Wissenschaften 44)

Kreutzmann, H. (1991): The Karakoram Highway – Impact of Road Construction on Mountain Societies. In: Modern Asian Studies 25, 4, pp. 711-736.

Kreutzmann, H. (1995): Sprachenvielfalt und regionale Differenzierung von Glaubensgemeinschaften im Hindukush-Karakorum. In: Erdkunde. Archiv für wissenschaftliche Geographie 49 (1995), pp. 106-121.

Kreutzmann, H. (1998): Sprachdifferenzierung in Ost-Hindukush und Karakorum. In: Kushew, V.V.; Luzhetskaia, N.L.; Rzehak, L.; Steblin-Kamensky, I.M. (eds.): Central Asia. Eastern Hindukush. St. Petersburg, Oriental Studies (1998), pp. 83-108.

Kreutzmann, H. (2005a): The Karakoram Landscape and the Recent History of the Northern Areas. In: Stephano Bianca (ed.): Karakoram: Hidden Treasures in the Northern Areas of Pakistan. Torino 2005, pp. 41-76.

Kreutzmann, H. (2005b): Linguistic diversity in space and time: A survey in the Eastern Hindukush and Karakoram. In: Himalayan Linguistics 4 (2005). pp. 1-24. Available at: *www.linguistics.ucsb.edu/HimalayanLinguistics/articles/2005/HLJ04_Kreutzmann.pdf* (Last update 15.11.2006)

Lorimer, D. L. R. (1915): Pashtu. Part I: Syntax of Colloquial Pashtu with chapters on the Persian and Indian Elements in the Modern Language. Oxford 1915

Munpool Meer Moonshee (1869): On Gilgit and Chitral. In: Proceedings of the Royal Geographical Society, Vol. XIII, Session 1868-9, Nos. I to V, London 1869, pp. 130-133.

Nejima, S., (1996): Diversity of Lineages in Ghizr, Northern Areas, Pakistan. In: Stellrecht, I. (ed.): Karakorum-Hindukush-Himalaya, Dynamics of Change, Part II – Culture Area Karakorum Scientific Studies, Vol 4. II, Köln 1998, pp. 405-416.

Population Census Organization of Pakistan. 1998 Census. Migrant Population by Place of Birth. Available at: *www.statpak.gov.pk/depts/pco/statistics/other_tables/migrant.pdf* (Accessed 15.04.2008).

Population Census Organization of Pakistan. 1998 Census. Population by Mother Tongue. Available at: *www.statpak.gov.pk/depts/pco/statistics/other_tables/pop_by_mother_tongue.pdf* (Accessed 15.04.2008).

Skjærvø, P. (1989): Pashto. In: Schmitt, R. (ed.): Compendium Linguarum Iranicarum. Wiesbaden 1989, pp. 384-410.

Sökefeld, M. (1997): Ein Labyrinth von Identitäten in Nordpakistan. Zwischen Landbesitz, Religion und Kaschmir-Konflikt. Köln 1997 (Culture Area Karakorum, Scientific Studies, Vol. 8).

Sökefeld, M. (1998a): On the Concept of 'Ethnic Group'. In: Stellrecht, I. (ed.): Karakorum-Hindukush-Himalaya, Dynamics of Change, Part II - Culture Area Karakorum, Scientific Studies, Vol 4.II, Köln 1998, pp. 383-403

Sökefeld, M. (1998b): Stereotypes and Boundaries: Pathan in Gilgit, Northern Pakistan. In: Kushew, V.V.; Luzhetskaia, N.L.; Rzehak, L.; Steblin-Kamensky, I.M. (eds.): Central Asia. Eastern Hindukush. St. Petersburg, Oriental Studies (1998), pp. 280-299.

Staley, J. (1966): Economy and Society in Dardistan: Traditional Systems and the Impact of Change. Manuscript. Lahore 1966.

Staley, J. (1969): Economy and Society in the High Mountains of Northern Pakistan. In: Modern Asian Studies, III, 3, Cambridge University Press, July 1969, pp. 225-243

Thakur Singh (1917): Assessment Report of the Gilgit Tahsil. Lahore 1917.

Weinreich, M. (2001): Die Pashto Sprecher des Karakorum. Zur Migrationsgeschichte einer ethno-linguistischen Minderheit. In: Iran and the Caucasus 5, Jerewan-Tehran 2001, pp. 285-302.

Weinreich, M. (2005): Pashto im Karakorum. Zur Sprachsituation und Sprache einer ethno-linguistischen Minderheit. In: Iran and the Caucasus 9.2, Brill, Leiden/Boston 2005, pp. 301-330.

Zoller, C. P. (2005): A Grammer and Dictionary of Indus Kohistani, Part I, Berlin 2005.

Status of Pashto and local languages among permanent Pashtun migrants

| No. | Father | | Mother | | Age | Informant | | | Wife | | Children | |
|---|---|---|---|---|---|---|---|---|---|---|---|---|
| | First language(s)[1] | Second language | First language(s) | Second language | | First language(s) | Second language | Language(s) used outside the home | First language(s) | Second language | First language(s) | Second language |
| 1 | PS | BL | PS | - | 15 | PS | BL | BL/UR | - | - | - | BL |
| 2 | PS | BL | PS | - | 17 | PS | BL | BL/UR | - | - | - | - |
| 3 | PS | SH | PS/SH | - | 18 | PS | SH | SH | - | - | - | - |
| 4 | PS | KW | KW | SH | 18 | KW/PS | SH/KW | KW | - | - | - | - |
| 5 | PS/KW | BL | KW | BL | 20 | PS | BL | BL | - | - | - | - |
| 6 | PS | SH | PS | SH | 20 | PS | SH | SH/PS | PS | SH | - | - |
| 7 | PS | SH | PS | - | 20 | PS | SH | SH/UR | PS | SH | - | - |
| 8 | PS | KW | PS | KW | 21 | PS | SH | SH | - | - | - | - |
| 9 | PS | - | PS | - | 21 | PS | KW | KW/PS | - | - | - | - |
| 10 | PS/SH | - | SH | PS | 22 | PS/SH | - | SH | - | - | - | - |
| 11 | PS | SH | PS | SH | 23 | PS | SH | SH/PS | PS | KW | PS | - |
| 12 | PS | SH | PS | - | 25 | PS | SH | SH/PS | PS | SH | PS | - |
| 13 | PS | SH | PS | - | 25 | PS | SH | SH/UR | PS | SH | PS | - |
| 14 | PS | SH | PS/SH | - | 25 | PS | SH | SH/UR | - | - | - | - |
| 15 | PS | KW/SH | PS | SH | 26 | PS | SH | SH | PS | - | PS | - |
| 16 | PS | SH | PS | - | 27 | PS | - | SH | PS | KW | PS | SH |
| 17 | PS | SH | SH | SH | 29 | SH/PS | - | SH | SH/PS | - | SH/PS | - |
| 18 | PS | SH | PS | - | 30 | PS | SH | SH | KW | BL | PS | - |
| 19 | PS | KW | KW | PS | 34 | KW/PS | - | KW | PS | BR | KW | BL |
| 20 | PS | UR | PS | KW | 36 | PS | BL | BL/UR | PS | BL | PS | BL |
| 21 | PS | KW | PS/KW | - | 40 | PS | KW | KW/PS | PS | KW | PS | KW |
| 22 | PS | SH | PS | - | 44 | PS | BL | BL/UR | PS/SH | - | PS | BL |
| 23 | PS | SH | SH | - | 47 | SH/PS | SH | SH/UR | SH | PS | PS | SH |
| 24 | PS | SH | PS | - | 50 | PS | - | SH/UR | PS | SH | PS | SH |
| 25 | PS | SH | SH | PS | 52 | PS/SH | - | SH | SH | - | PS | SH |
| 26 | PS | SH | SH | - | 52 | SH/PS | - | SH | SH | - | SH | UR |
| 27 | PS | SH | PS | SH | 55 | SH | SH | SH | SH | PS | PS | SH |
| 28 | PS | - | PS | KW | 60 | PS | BL | BL/UR | PS | BL | PS | BL |
| 29 | PS/SH | - | SH | - | 70 | SH/PS | - | SH | SH/PS | - | SH/PS | - |
| 30 | PS | SH | PS | SH | 75 | PS | KW | SH | PS | SH | PS | SH |

[1] As 'first language(s)' we consider the language(s) learnt from the parents during early childhood. 'Second language(s)' are those which are acquired outside the family. Informants were requested to name the second language most frequently used by them as well as the two languages most frequently spoken by them outside their homes. The information concerning the languages used by the mother and wife is exclusively based on statements made by the male household members. PS stands for Pashto, SH for Shina, KW for Khowar, BL for Balti, BR for Burushaski and UR for Urdu.

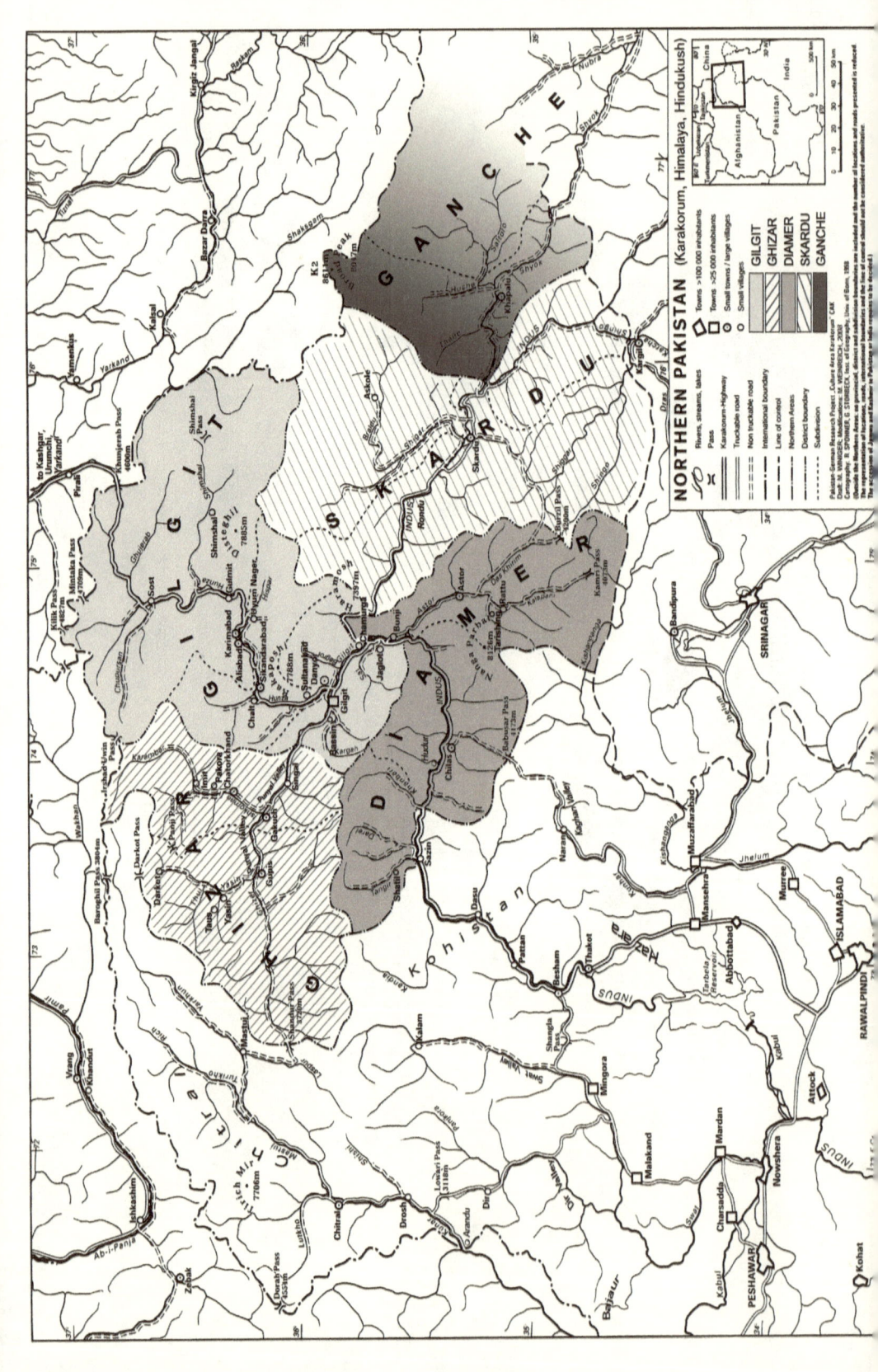

www.ingramcontent.com/pod-product-compliance
Lightning Source LLC
Chambersburg PA
CBHW021956290426
44108CB00012B/1096